Paper Tigers
A Christian Woman's Guide To Overcoming

By Dr. Lianne S. Kernan

Paper Tigers
A Christian Woman's Guide To Overcoming

Copyright © 2021 by Dr. Lianne S. Kernan

All rights reserved.

No part of this publication may be reproduced, distributed or transmitted in any form or by any means - including photocopying, recording or other electronic or mechanical methods - without the prior written permission of the author (except in the case of brief quotations embodied in critical reviews, sermons, lessons, articles and certain other noncommercial uses permitted by copyright and fair usage law). For permission requests, please email the author at the address below:

lianne@usd21.org

SoldOut Press International

Editor-in-Chief – Dr. Kip McKean

ISBN: 9798703442050

Contents

Acknowledgments 6

Foreword by Dr. Elena Garcia McKean 12

Introduction 17

Paper Tiger One: Sarah's Doubt 24

Paper Tiger Two: Rebekah's Desire For Control 45

Paper Tiger Three: Rachel's Rivalry 79

Paper Tiger Four: Lot's Wife's Longing For The World 106

Paper Tiger Five: The Bleeding Woman's Suffering 139

Paper Tiger Six: The Adulterous Woman's Guilty Feelings 160

Paper Tiger Seven: Naomi's Bitterness 174

Epilogue 210

Contact The Author 213

Acknowledgments

This book would have never come to be if it had not been for God, who guided me to the truth and saved my soul. Thank you for having mercy on me and giving me a life of faith, hope and love.

Thank you to my best friend, the love of my life, my leader, the perfect man for me in every way, my husband, Tim. You looked at me and saw what I could become, not who I was. I love your zeal for God and your desire to advance and protect the church.

Indeed, like the prophet Ezekiel, God has given you a forehead of flint. While it is not always easy for you, you always stay focused on God, positive and motivated. I want you to know that I am proud of you. I want you to know that I believe in you. I want you to know that I am by your side on this crazy roller coaster ride, for better or worse. Thank you for the gift of two incredible sons and for helping me be the best woman of God that I can be.

Thank you to my two precious sons, Tim Junior and David. Mommy is so very grateful for both of you. You love Daddy and me so much and always inspire us to love God! I want to make you proud of me!

Tim Junior, thank you for being so loving and helpful. Thank you for your thoughtful accountability! When I would come in to be with David and you at bedtime, you would say, "Mommy, shouldn't you be working on your book?" Thank you for always keeping me motivated!

David, thank you for being so patient with me as I wrote this book. You would always come and give me a big hug to encourage me, and I am so grateful to you. Thank you for waiting "just a little longer" for your snacks while I finished writing a thought!

Thank you, Kip and Elena McKean, for your incredible faith and your perseverance. What would we do, and where would we be without you? You have known me for 15 years of my 21 years as a disciple! I owe you a debt of gratitude that I can never repay.

Elena, you are an extraordinary role model of a woman who fixes her eyes on Jesus and does not allow herself to get distracted by the wind and waves of life, hardship and heartache. You are a tremendous example of grace under pressure and of nobility no matter what is going on around you. You have taught me so much! Thank you for giving me your heart and your trust. If I can be half the disciple that you are, then I will call myself blessed.

Kip, you are the father in the faith to Tim and me. Thank you for loving my husband and believing in him, for being his friend and coach. Thank you for your constant encouragement and those gentle but "life-giving rebukes." Tim and I so appreciate your heartfelt concern for the spiritual wellbeing of Junior and David.

Mom, thank you for bringing me into this world, raising my sister and me, and teaching me to believe in God from a young age. You sacrificed so much and worked so hard for us, more than I am sure I will ever know. Thank you for supporting me at my baptism on January 29, 1997 when I discovered true discipleship.

Dad, thank you for becoming a disciple in my pre-teen years and for having that conversation on the living room couch in Montreal in 1996 that I will never forget. You showed me James 4 and urged me to have the right motives in life and love. As a result of our talk, I studied the Bible and was baptized at 19 years old, avoiding so many of the dreadful consequences of being in the world in my 20s.

A heartfelt thank you to all the women used by God to study the Bible with me and baptize me! Thank you, Brigitte, for showing me love and Tamara for being a big sister that I could follow. Thank you, Jenny, for being my first mentor in the church and teaching me so much and Karen, for counting the cost with me. Thank you, Anne, for being the Women's Ministry Leader who led the study that showed me how to go from the darkness to the light. Thank you to Gillianne for being family.

Thank you to Ghislain, Kobi, Brendan and Prosper for studying the Bible with my awesome husband. Thanks, of course, to the mighty Portland Church in 2004 for reminding us of our first love. Thanks to Steve and Amy for hosting us every year during the Jubilee. I will never forget that dinner at your house. It was a turning point for us. Thanks to Vic Sr. and Sonia for treating us like family during those auspicious times.

Thank you, John and Emma Causey for being by our side as together we led the church in Los Angeles. What a noble pursuit of the "ancient paths" those days were! I love you both so much!

John, thank you for teaching Tim and me to grow into our role as the City of Angels Church Leaders! You are a coach that has helped us navigate many storms with dignity, nobility, honor and faith. Thank you for helping me remember that I am not an evangelist, but to love my role and teach me what it means to "stay in my lane!"

Emma, thank you for mentoring me and for being a safe place. You have helped me mature and grow in my leadership, not being afraid to laugh at the days to come! Thank you for helping me to surrender to God, as well as to yield to who He wants me to be! You were sent by God when we needed you the most. You will never know how grateful we are for you and your precious family.

Jason and Sarah Dimitry, thank you for loving us and for being there from the beginning. Thank you, Ricky and Coleen Challinor, for your abiding friendship. We are so proud of you and your leadership of the mighty Metro Manila Church! Thank you, Jared and Rachel McGee for your undying loyalty.

Thank you, Nick and Denise Bordieri, Tony and Therese Untalan, and Michael and Sharon Kirchner, who have helped us and been lifelong friends and confidants. Thank you, Ryan and Iyonna Keenan for your diligence in administration for the City of Angels Church and the Tribe World Sector.

Thank you to our fellow partners in the gospel all around the world: Raul and Lynda Moreno of São Paulo, Andrew and Patrique Smellie of Johannesburg, Michael and Michele Williamson of London, Joe and Kerry Willis of Sydney, Cory and Jee Blackwell of San Diego, Oleg and Aliona Sirotkin of Kyiv, and Matt and Helen Sullivan of Miami. Let us continuously champion a unified movement that evangelizes the world.

Thank you, Kernan Clan past and present: Megan, Michelle, Maria, Daniela, Jessie, Mialynn, Heidi, Keirra, Haley, Devon, Xanthe, Dylan, Jazmin and Michelle. You have helped us more than you will ever know and you have seen all of our flaws and still love us. Thank you, precious City of Angels Shieldmaidens. You inspire me and are the joy of my heart and one of the many great hopes for the church. You make me a better leader.

Thank you to the LA Super Region Leaders: RD and April Baker, Brian and Joaly Carr, Richie and Elizabeth McDonnell, and Joey and Karen Gregory for being the closest of family to Tim and me.

Thank you to our beloved City of Angels Church Staff for your hearts to lift up our arms and be our fellow workers in Christ! I am grateful for every single one of you and for how you desire to see God's great people taken care of in Los Angeles.

Thank you to the dynamic church leaders in the Pacific Rim Tribe World Sector and all the dedicated disciples. Please pray that I can learn more and more every day how to be an even better Women's Ministry Leader as we work side by side in this great commission: To seek and save as many as possible!

Thank you to Chris Adams, Cheryl Chin, Ashley Sarkodie, Rachel McGee, Julie Clark, Jennifer Watkins and Karen Gregory. You have all done a phenomenal job helping to edit, and I am so grateful for your sacrifice of time. Of course, thanks for the hours of the "final three edits," dear Kip!

Lastly, thank you to everyone who has encouraged me to persevere through your often humorous social media posts. I pray that this book will aid in your pilgrimage to please our Father in Heaven... and one day join Him.

Foreword
Dr. Elena Garcia McKean

The COVID-19 Pandemic has impacted everyone around the globe, most believe for the worse. Yet this lengthy pause in our lives has allowed the author the precious time needed to write the ground-breaking book: *Paper Tigers - A Christian Women's Guide To Overcoming*. I do believe this book alongside the growing library of the SoldOut Press International Publishing House is changing the world… for immediate and everlasting good! Indeed, Lianne S. Kernan - the gifted author - shares many spiritual lessons and crucial insights through the Biblical accounts of seven courageous women: Sarah, Rebekah, Rachel, Lot's Wife, the Bleeding Woman, the Adulterous Woman and Naomi. In each chapter, Lianne vulnerably shares from her life to illustrate the dangers and opportunities in wrestling with each "paper tiger."

God brought this young, vibrant Canadian woman into my life at the First Portland World Missions Jubilee in June 2004. At the time, Lianne was 27 years old and married to her awesome husband Tim for only eight months. The Kernans had traveled all the way from their hurting "home church" in Montreal, Canada to Portland, Oregon believing that this was their "last hope." They came seeking spiritual revival for themselves and their "home church." Tim and Lianne humbly asked Kip and me for "discipling," as well as to help the Montreal International Church of Christ. Sadly, though the Montreal Church "turned its back" on our attempts of help, Tim and Lianne never faltered in their Biblical convictions on discipling as a command of God, Central Leadership as the plan of God, and the vision of the evangelization of the nations in this generation as the dream of God.

In early 2007, Kip and I invited Tim and Lianne to join us on the Portland Mission Team to Los Angeles. They arrived from Toronto in time for the May 6, 2007 City of Angels International Christian Church Inaugural Service. Incredibly, we all stood in awe of God that day as the 42 disciples on the mission team saw 324 in attendance… and so God's new SoldOut Discipling Movement officially began with Tim and Lianne at our side. Since, the International Christian Church was in its infancy, there was only four months of full-time support for the Kernans. Therefore, Kip thought that they could "raise their support" by initiating a remnant group in London, England. Amazingly, this they did in September 2007, and in turn, God blessed them with "Tim Junior" in 2008!

During their time in the New Movement, Tim and Lianne have served the Lord and His great people in London, Toronto, Paris, Chennai and of course Los Angeles. While in LA in 2011, God blessed them with their second son David! As well, it was during Lianne's "LA days" that we worked together very closely on building the Women's Ministry, especially Women's Days and in the International College of Christian Ministries. Through these efforts, Lianne not only became a terrific organizer, but an outstanding Women's Ministry Leader! Lianne has grown so much in her relationship with the Lord - so evident in her radiance and confidence - that she has become one of my top five women speakers… with no number one.

In late 2015, the challenges of leading a fast-growing, global family of discipling congregations and the City of Angels Church began to be too much for Kip and me. In handing over the leadership of the City of Angels Church on December 13, 2015, Kip shared this passage about "his" Timothy, *"I have no one else like [Tim]… For everyone looks out for his own interests, not those of Jesus Christ. But [Tim] has proved himself, because as a son with their father he has served with me in the work of the gospel."* Following, I echoed this same familial bond with Lianne as mother and dear daughter in the faith. I also expressed that Lianne was a Proverbs 11:16 woman, *"A kindhearted woman gains respect."* As expressed in the 2015 Disney Movie *Cinderella,* "There is a great power in kindness coupled with courage."

Then, Tim and Lianne shared their hearts for us. Lianne's sharing moved me to tears. Lianne likewise was weeping as she shared that her heart for me was the same as Ruth had for Naomi. Lianne's undying loyalty has been so like Ruth's, as expressed in Ruth 1:16-17, *"Don't urge me to leave you or to turn back from you. Where you go I will go, and where you stay I will stay. Your people will be my people and your God my God. Where you die I will die, and there I will be buried. May the Lord deal with me, be it ever so severely, if anything but death separates you and me."* Our trust in Tim and Lianne leading the "mother church" of the Movement has more than gone *"beyond anything that we could have asked or imagined."* (Ephesians 3:20) Under the Kernans' inspirational leadership, hundreds of strong leaders - both men and women - have been raised up and sent out from LA on mission teams around the world to Lagos, Dubai, Guam, Phnom Penh, Chicago, San Diego, Manila, Portland, Tampa, Atlanta, Toronto and Washington DC, just to name a few! Lianne has become a mother in the faith to sons and daughters across the nations!

With the completion of this book - Lianne's ICCM Doctoral Dissertation - she became only the second woman to receive the prestigious ICCM Doctorate Degree. Congratulations dearest sister and daughter! Congratulations, Dr. Lianne Shannon Kernan! I look forward to reading many more of your insightful, impassioned and intriguing books… maybe *Paper Tigers Book Two?* And to God be all the glory!

Dr. Elena Garcia McKean
Los Angeles, California
January 1, 2021

The Hand That Rocks The Cradle
William Ross Wallace (1819-1881)

Blessings on the hand of women!
Angels guard its strength and grace.
In the palace, cottage, hovel,
Oh, no matter where the place;
Would that never storms assailed it,
Rainbows ever gently curled,
For the hand that rocks the cradle
Is the hand that rules the world.
Infancy's the tender fountain,
Power may with beauty flow,
Mothers first to guide the streamlets,
From them souls unresting grow -
Grow on for the good or evil,
Sunshine streamed or evil hurled,
For the hand that rocks the cradle
Is the hand that rules the world.
Woman, how divine your mission,
Here upon our natal sod;
Keep-oh, keep the young heart open
Always to the breath of God!
All true trophies of the ages
Are from mother-love impearled,
For the hand that rocks the cradle
Is the hand that rules the world.
Blessings on the hand of women!
Fathers, sons and daughters cry,
And the sacred song is mingled
With the worship in the sky -
Mingles where no tempest darkens,
Rainbows evermore are hurled;
For the hand that rocks the cradle
Is the hand that rules the world.

Introduction

"She is clothed with strength and dignity; she can laugh at the days to come. She speaks with wisdom, and faithful instruction is on her tongue." (Proverbs 31: 25-26)

This Scripture brings to mind a fascinating Chinese saying, "All seemingly powerful enemies are merely Paper Tigers."[1] The term "Paper Tiger" is the literal translation of a Chinese phrase that means "something or someone who appears powerful but is in fact harmless." With God, all our problems are mere Paper Tigers, allowing us to laugh at the days to come. I appreciate the quote for what it is. I believe it relates to the challenges we face as women. The worst nightmares we have are mere "Paper Tigers" in the face of the power of God.

Women have a God-given and captivating ability to transform a room when we enter it. We can make life good. We can inspire, lighten and cheer any situation.

We can enrich men and children's lives and encourage them to do bold things and be better. Our ability to influence is powerful. We have birthed and raised all of the most influential people in history. This gift to give life and sustain the next generation is from God. The most remarkable example of this is Mary, as God chose her to bear His son and bring a revolution that forever impacted our world.

---

[1] https://www.marxists.org/reference/archive/mao/selected-works/volume-5/mswv5_70.htm

Instead of honoring women's unique strength and power, Satan's effort is to rid our society of gender differences, as if they are a terrible thing. In the following seven chapters, women will crumple up the Paper Tigers of Doubt, the Desire for Control, and Rivalry. We will tear apart the Paper Tigers of Longing for the World, Suffering, Guilty Feelings and Bitterness.

With every obstacle, there are two roads that we can take. While God wants to offer us His solutions, Satan is also trying to "solve" our problems for us. Indeed, the world has surged forward to empower a new generation of women. Businesses benefit from an increased pool of laborers as women enter the workforce in a way in which they never have. Retailers benefit from female spending power.

More and more women are rising to fill influential roles in government, business and management. Women are using their God-given strengths and unique talents to advance every significant area of science and discovery. Nevertheless, despite these progressive developments, in a 2008 study, researchers noticed a decline in "female happiness" from the 1970's onward.[2] Some studies have revealed that many women are now more alone, more overwhelmed, more overworked, more indebted, less powerful, and less happy than ever before.

---

[2] https://law.yale.edu/sites/default/files/documents/pdf/Intellectual_Life/Stevenson_ParadoxDecliningFemaleHappiness_Dec08.pdf

The truth is that there is little good without God. Every effort to liberate humanity that was not centered on God ended up enslaving us. Feminism began as a way to improve society's outlook on women and our role in society. However, the further our society strayed from God, the more twisted women's lives have become.

Though Feminism initially strove to empower and promote healthy equality between men and women, it has now led to a victim mentality, bitterness and competitiveness with the very people who need nurturing the most - men. It has stifled the wise, kind and gentle side of our character that makes us so essential and so necessary in this world. The more women fixate on themselves, our desperately needed impact on the planet is muted.

Today, there is a destructive and toxic belief that women must be more masculine to be more powerful as if being like a man makes a woman better. God put women on the Earth because it was ***"not good"*** for man to be alone. (Genesis 2:18) Biblically, therefore, women are essential to make the world "good!"

It is undeniable that throughout history, there have been godless men who, out of insecurity and fear of women's power, have been manipulated by Satan to oppress and diminish us. Satan knows that we are a threat. As a reaction to the abuse women have endured, extreme Feminism seeks to "right the ship." Instead, it is "sinking the ship" as we descend into more and more depravity, self-absorption and confusion.

The desire for retribution and justice has caused us to "pendulum swing" towards strange new societal models where roles are reversing and spinning out of control. Instead, we must return to the true Women's Liberation Movement, which is Jesus' Movement. We must revive the powerful female models who are examples to us in the Bible.

God, through Jesus, created women. (John 1:3) We were created to be influential leaders and co-heirs of the Kingdom of God. Therefore, it could be said that there has never been a true feminist like Jesus! He desires for women to be empowered, free and active. However, these qualities come from inside, not just outside. Our strength does not come from reacting to wrongdoing. So much of the drive behind the secular female empowerment movement has become reactionary. As mentioned before, it is rooted in a victim mentality and self-pity. While understandable, as Christians, we believe this is unacceptable. A victim mentality will never change the world for the better. Jesus, when mistreated did not retaliate nor make any threats. (1 Peter 2:23) Like the Savior we follow, we must have a revolutionary mindset to impact this world.

In the following chapters, Paper Tiger-fighting women in the Bible will teach us how to overcome our fears and insecurities through both their victories and failures. As each woman navigates her way through the turbulent waters, we will observe her convictions. Each woman will provide us with an example we can follow or avoid in our everyday lives and ministries. We will cleanse ourselves of confusion, nourish ourselves on the Word of God, and learn to fulfill God's will for our lives in this generation. As women and fellow heirs to God's promises, we know the world cannot change without us.

The beauty of our kind is that as women we relieve and expel loneliness, discouragement and confusion. We were never designed to live in them. We have the power to bring the light of God into the home, the church, the community and the entire world. We provide dedicated and godly partnerships and remind men that it is good to be alive, to hope and to love, to be the light of the world. We lead and train our children. Indeed, the hand that rocks the cradle is the hand that rules the world.

If about half of the planet's population is female, close to 50 percent of the world's problems would be solved if women would be committed to upholding the Bible's standard. Implied, of course, is that the other 50 percent of the world's problems will be solved when men decide to do the same. That, however, is not the focus of my writing.

As women of faith, action and sound Biblical convictions, our doubt, need for control, anxiety, intimidation, isolation, shame and succumbing to emotional and spiritual fatigue can be overcome. We can be strong women without needing to become masculine. We can then work with our fathers, male peers, husbands, brothers and sons, as respected and dearly loved mothers, partners, wives, sisters and daughters.

Every Christian woman should have the following Biblical lessons imprinted on their hearts and minds so that we can be genuinely free and please God. Start turning the pages and watch your life and the lives of everyone around you change. They will change as we recommit ourselves to God's purpose for women, just as He intended from the very beginning.

"Doubt kills more dreams than failure ever will."

Suzy Kassem

Paper Tiger One
Sarah's Doubt

The Expulsion of Hagar and Ishmael
Adriaen van der Werff (1696 - 1697)

God also said to Abraham, "As for Sarai your wife, you are no longer to call her Sarai; her name will be Sarah. I will bless her and will surely give you a son by her. I will bless her so that she will be the mother of nations; kings of peoples will come from her."

> *Abraham fell facedown; he laughed and said to himself, "Will a son be born to a man a hundred years old? Will Sarah bear a child at the age of ninety?" And Abraham said to God, "If only Ishmael might live under your blessing!"*
>
> *Then God said, "Yes, but your wife Sarah will bear you a son, and you will call him Isaac. I will establish my covenant with him as an everlasting covenant for his descendants after him. And as for Ishmael, I have heard you: I will surely bless him; I will make him fruitful and will greatly increase his numbers. He will be the father of twelve rulers, and I will make him into a great nation. But my covenant I will establish with Isaac, whom Sarah will bear to you by this time next year." When He had finished speaking with Abraham, God went up from him.* (Genesis 17:15-22)

This Scripture records the celebrated interaction between God and Abraham regarding Sarah, one of the most important women in the Bible. Her original name Sarai means "my princess," but her God-given name Sarah means "princess of the multitudes," simply put "princess of the nations." After all, Sarah was the Matriarch of God's chosen people and the first Hebrew woman.[3]

---

[3] https://www.Biblegateway.com/resources/all-women-Bible/Sarah-Sarai-Sara

Her husband Abram, later Abraham, was the tenth descendant of Noah and was born in Ur of the Chaldees, thought to be southern Mesopotamia, modern-day Iraq.[4] God called Abram while in Ur before he settled with his father Terah in Haran.[5] In Haran, Terah died. (Genesis 11:32) Abram then continued his calling from God to go to Canaan with his wife Sarai and his nephew Lot.

In Genesis 17, God told Abram - who was 99 years old at that time - that he would no longer be called Abram, meaning "exalted father," but instead Abraham, "father of many nations." (Genesis 17:5) However, the promise of becoming the father of many nations was through a son to be born through Sarah, not Hagar. At that time, Abraham seemed fully persuaded that God had the power to do what He had promised. (Romans 4:21) However, in Genesis 17 when Sarah was 89 years old, she had a more difficult time seeing past her current reality: She was barren.

Sarai/Sarah was a stunningly attractive woman. Abram said of her, *"I know what a beautiful woman you are."* (Genesis 12:11) Indeed when *"Abram came to Egypt, the Egyptians saw that Sarai was a very beautiful woman."* (Genesis 12:14) However, while her feminine body and beautiful features would most likely have suggested fertility, she could not bear Abram a child.

---

[4]https://www.britannica.com/place/Chaldea
[5]Acts 7:2-3

In Genesis 18, three strangers appeared in Abraham's camp. Abraham hurried to meet them and fell prostrate before them. This behavior is described as "first falling on one's knees, and then inclining the head forwards until it touches the ground."[6] According to the *Pulpit Commentary,* this manner of greeting is reserved for royalty. Fascinatingly, Abraham then offered the three visitors water to wash their feet, shelter under a tree, and eat a sumptuous meal. The level of hospitality shown to these strangers reveals the generous and kind heart of the host. It also strongly alludes to the possibility that Abraham knew that these were no ordinary men. As Abraham was hosting them, they delivered a message and had this interaction with Sarah.

"Where is your wife Sarah?" they asked him.

"There, in the tent," he said.

Then one of them said, "I will surely return to you about this time next year, and Sarah your wife will have a son."

Now Sarah was listening at the entrance to the tent, which was behind him. Abraham and Sarah were already very old, and Sarah was past the age of childbearing. So Sarah laughed to herself as she thought, "After I am worn out

---

[6]http://Biblehub.com/commentaries/pulpit/genesis/18.htm

and my lord is old, will I now have this pleasure?"

Then the Lord said to Abraham, "Why did Sarah laugh and say, 'Will I really have a child, now that I am old?' Is anything too hard for the Lord? I will return to you at the appointed time next year, and Sarah will have a son."

Sarah was afraid, so she lied and said, "I did not laugh."

But He said, "Yes, you did laugh." (Genesis 18:9-15)

One of the visitors informed Abraham that he and his wife would have their first child by this time the next year. Sarah, hiding at the entrance to the tent while eavesdropping, let her skepticism bubble to the surface. She began to laugh. The laughter denoted disbelief and doubt, as she considered the possibility of having a child of her own at 90 years old.

Sarah's desire for children most likely produced an emptiness within her. Perhaps as a result of a sense of purpose that had never been fulfilled to be "fruitful." However, nestled deep within that heartbreaking emptiness, had grown the Paper Tiger of Doubt.

One of the visitors was the Lord, possibly the preincarnate Christ, who asked Abraham why Sarah laughed, knowing that she *"was listening at the entrance of the tent."* (Genesis 18:10) Upon being confronted for laughing, Sarah denied the charge. The *Pulpit Commentary* argues that her denial was brought about by realizing that one of the visitors was the Lord, so Sarah felt very guilty.[7] Being barren for so long had made her cynical and skeptical.

Skepticism is a very unattractive trait. When we allow our world view to be clouded by negativity, it can steal our fruitfulness as disciples and also our power as women. Louis Pasteur said, "Do not let yourself be tainted with a barren skepticism." Skepticism will kill the fruits of the Spirit and will make us spiritually barren.

Doubt can be an instinctive emotion. The definition of the English word "doubt" is "to be uncertain about; consider questionable or unlikely; hesitate to believe."[8] The Hebrew word is "taraph," which means to be "torn in pieces."

Giving pause and considering our situation can, in some cases, save our lives. We may need to cross the street, but we may pause and proceed with caution and avoid a car because we cannot fully see around the corner. Doubt is there for a purpose and has a place in everyday life, but doubt will hurt us spiritually when we doubt God and His direction.

While Sarai/Sarah's disbelief in hearing God's promise is not very surprising, it is unacceptable. She had been conditioned by many years of barrenness. She knew "beyond a shadow of a doubt" that she could not conceive naturally. Since this constant narrative was going on inside

---

[7] http://Biblehub.com/genesis/18-15.htm
[8] http://www.dictionary.com/browse/doubt?s=t

her head, there was not much room for faith. Instead of trusting in God's promise to Abram, Sarai had already taken matters into her own hands. (Genesis 15:4-5)

Even though God Almighty had promised that Abram would be a mighty nation and that Abram and Sarai would have a son, Sarai doubted. (Genesis 15:4) Before the three strangers' visit, Sarai took Hagar, her Egyptian handmaid, and gave her to Abram as a concubine to bring God's promise to fruition by her express design.

> *Now Sarai, Abram's wife, had borne him no children. But she had an Egyptian slave named Hagar; so she said to Abram, "The Lord has kept me from having children. Go, sleep with my slave; perhaps I can build a family through her."*
>
> *Abram agreed to what Sarai said. So after Abram had been living in Canaan ten years, Sarai his wife took her Egyptian slave Hagar and gave her to her husband to be his wife. He slept with Hagar, and she conceived.*
>
> *When she knew she was pregnant, she began to despise her mistress. Then Sarai said to Abram, "You are responsible for the wrong I am suffering. I put my slave in your arms, and now that she knows she is pregnant, she despises me. May the Lord judge between you and me."*

> *"Your slave is in your hands," Abram said. "Do with her whatever you think best." Then Sarai mistreated Hagar; so she fled from her.*
> (Genesis 16:1-6)

Sarai's and Abram's choices created a terrible conflict. Abram's second wife, Hagar, accomplished what Sarai could not by becoming pregnant. The bond between parents expecting their first child is unique. As the one observing this happiness from the outside, Sarai became the subject of Hagar's disdain.

According to the customs of the time, Hagar would now be seen as "superior" and "more favored by God" than Sarai. In Sarai's pain, she retaliated by treating Hagar quite harshly. Hagar then fled to the desert with her child. Though not originally part of the plan, God promised to make Ishmael - Hagar's son - into a great nation. (Genesis 16:10)

Sarah's faithless actions and doubt, as well as Abraham's acquiescence, created enemies for Israel,

> *The Angel of the Lord also said to [Hagar]: "You are now pregnant and you will give birth to a son. You shall name him Ishmael, for the Lord has heard of your misery. He will be a wild donkey of a man; his hand will be against everyone and everyone's hand against him, and he will live in hostility with all his brothers."*
> (Genesis 16:11-12)

Though Hagar and Ishmael returned, 13 years later, they are cast out by Abraham. Ishmael must have had a challenging time in his upbringing. Imagine being expelled from your father's home with your mother, who really was the unfortunate victim of another woman's doubt. Imagine then being replaced as heir by your younger brother. What would that have done to shape Ishmael's view of himself? When children feel rejected by a parent, it can put a deep resentment in them. The bitterness can quickly turn into aggression and a "being at odds" with everyone around them. We see the Genesis 16:12 prophecy's truth, as Abrahams's and Sarah's actions resulted in the lasting feud between the Arabs and Hebrews to this day.

The Expulsion of Hagar
Gustave Dore (1877)

For years in Sarai's and Abram's marriage, their pattern was to deal with difficult situations in a worldly way by taking matters into their own hands. Sarai agreed to go along with Abram's suggestion to lie to Pharaoh about not being Abram's wife but only his sister. (Genesis 12:10-20) She agreed again in Genesis 20. Sadly in Genesis 12, we can infer that Sarai was intimate with the Pharaoh because God punished Pharaoh. (Genesis 12:17) In contrast in Genesis 20, God Himself spoke that nothing physical happened between Abimelech and Sarah. (Genesis 20:6) God had a more excellent plan for Sarah that He was working on, but Sarah needed to be pruned to become who she was meant to be: Mother of the people of God.

Some may relate more to Hagar than to Sarah. We are regularly involved in helping others, serving them, and lifting them to make them great. Maybe God has blessed us more than others, and the resulting praise has made us think more of ourselves than we should. We begin to think of ourselves as better than others. We may not even realize it, but a feeling of superiority begins to creep in, and we begin to look down on anyone that is not getting the "results" that we are.

Instead of helping other disciples experience victory, we allow disdain to creep into our hearts slowly. It becomes more about how "awesome" we are and not about how amazing God is. This "spiritual narcissism" can cloud our judgment and, in turn, lead to conflict between disciples as it did for Sarai and Hagar.

Unhealthy competition breeds an environment in the women's ministry of "cattiness" and negativity. Similar to

Hagar, some scoff and despise those who are struggling. Eventually, instead of the church uniting people as it should, it becomes a place where women are divided and unproductive. More on this later in *Paper Tiger Three: Rachel's Rivalry.* Suffice it to say, doubt will lead to friction between disciples.

I have had my struggles with doubt. In 1997 after studying the Bible for two weeks, I decided to give my life to God and became a Christian according to the Word of God. I was baptized as a disciple of Jesus in Montreal, Canada. Those first three years as a true Christian were some of the best times of my life. As a "baby Christian," I would open my Bible every day and read the Proverbs. I remember reading those Proverbs for the first time and being so inspired by them.

I had learned to share my faith with friends and strangers, study the Bible with women, and see them become disciples. I will never forget the wonder of those early days: the pure encouragement group dates, the camping trips, the prayer walks and the newness of learning all about God. I am so grateful for those times.

By year six of being a disciple, however, my faith began to weaken. In 2003, the Montreal International Church of Christ - Tim's and my home congregation - started to go through very significant changes in ***"life and doctrine."*** (1 Timothy 4:16) Around the world, all of the International Churches of Christ (ICOC) were drastically affected by the "new direction:" Bible Talks, one on one discipling, and even evangelism all became optional. Confusion poured into our church. Life suddenly changed for Tim and me, but we held on spiritually through a very tumultuous first year of marriage. Saddest of all, I became spiritually lukewarm.

The Author and her husband on their first date as a dating couple!

In 2004, knowing that our beloved Montreal Church and we needed renewal, Tim began to call other ministers to reach out for help. No one concretely offered any solutions or support. Then one night, Tim called Kip McKean - the former leader of the entire ICOC and the then leader of the Portland ICOC. We did not know him or Elena personally, so it was a final effort to find out what was happening on behalf of my husband. After a long conversation with my husband, Kip invited us to come to Portland for their World Missions Jubilee in June 2004 to see what God had been doing in the Portland Church. I was apprehensive due to my spiritual acedia, but I decided to follow my husband, knowing that I needed help.

The McKeans and Kernans met at the First Portland World Missions Jubilee in June 2004!

What we saw was so inspiring. On the first night of our arrival, we stayed with a family in the Portland Church. I will never forget our first dinner with them. As we shared about how much we had drifted spiritually and were hurting in our marriage, the husband got up, went into the other room, and returned with a Bible. He sat back down and flipped through the pages, and gave us spiritual counsel and advice. Tim and I could not believe it. This family did not know us, yet because we were disciples, they unashamedly called us to the Bible's standard. It was at that moment we knew we needed to be with this inspiring group of disciples.

We had initially decided to move right away, but after a discussion with our church leader, we decided to go back to Canada and help our home congregation. God worked incredibly, and the Montreal Church decided to seek renewal along with other disciples around the world, also seeking revival in the "Portland Movement." I felt during that time that our church began to flourish once more. It was such an exciting time.

In 2006, doubt returned to the Montreal Church Leadership, and they disassociated itself with Kip, Elena and the Portland Church. I believe that when Satan causes disunity through past hurts and misunderstandings, he turns even the most well-meaning people against one another. Indeed, Satan had a significant victory in the Montreal Church, and we were too weak and inexperienced to be of any help.

For Tim and me to return to our former state of lukewarmness was not an option. We believed in what was being done in Portland and had seen the positive effects in Montreal, so we chose to stay in the "embryonic" SoldOut Discipling Movement.

Being in Portland reminded me of when I was first baptized and made me believe that I could get spiritually healthy again. At this time I believe God opened an opportunity for Tim and me to move to Toronto, Canada, and we established a remnant group of the Portland Movement.

I will never forget Tim and I moving to Toronto. Although our leaving the Montreal Church and establishing the Toronto Remnant Group was in no way executed in the perfect way, we did not regret our decision to move on. We were emotionally and spiritually weary. The last few months in Montreal had taken its toll on our faith. Sometimes I doubted that God could turn around my spiritual condition.

Those were very dark days, some of the darkest spiritually that I have ever experienced.

Despite these events, I knew that the Bible was still true, and God was still sovereign. While I was fragile spiritually, I wanted to be like the examples of committed women found in the Bible. However, as we began again in Toronto, I remember doubting that I could be fruitful. Thank God for my husband, who would say, "Just stand beside me, and I will share my faith for both of us." Sometimes I could not even do that.

I began working at a secular job in Toronto and wrestled with doubt and despair. It is an odd thing to know the good you ought to do but feel too weak and alone to do it. I had a partner in my husband, but I did not have a sister in Christ to be my "partner in the gospel."

I fought with that pressure to make a disciple in my soul daily. The doubt followed me to work, on the subway, in the stores, everywhere I went. It was not imposed or forced upon me by anyone because there was no one around. It came from within because I knew what the Bible said… Nevertheless, I was weak.

During those early days, the only strength I had was to pray to God to help me make just one disciple. I so badly wanted someone that I could disciple, someone who would be zealous for God with me. Like Sarah, I had been spiritually barren for so long, and so the idea of baptizing someone began to seem impossible. All I could do was to pray to God to **"strengthen [my] feeble arms and weak knees"** and share my faith on the way to work. (Hebrews 12:12)

It just so happened the one disciple that had followed us to Toronto, a teen from Tim's previous ministry in Montreal, shared his faith on the subway with a young woman. The young woman was encouraged by the encounter, and after exchanging numbers, they parted ways. Days later, this same woman entered the workplace of that disciple, who at the time was working at a fast-food restaurant. She was immediately struck by the "coincidence" of seeing him once more. Of course, it was not a coincidence, but the hand of God. (Acts 17:26-27) The teen challenged her to attend our church that coming Sunday, and the young woman enthusiastically agreed.

That Sunday, she came to our little church service, and was deeply inspired by Tim's sermon. She quickly realized that the love of our small group of disciples had impacted her so much. (John 13:34-35) As I sat next to her, I knew what I should do. After all, I had been taught as a young disciple that faith without deeds is dead, so it was vital to ask the visitor if she wanted to study the Bible. I prayed that God would give me the strength to speak with her once service was over, even though doubt was preying on my faith.

As the church service concluded, I turned to her, and we began talking. During the conversation, I felt the Holy Spirit's prompting, urging me to ask if she would like to study the Bible. I asked half-heartedly. I fully expected her to decline. Imagine my surprise when she exuberantly agreed!

She said that she was in the process of seeking after God and had gone to church after church looking for the truth and for true Christians to teach her the Bible. She would attend a church service, make her way to the front of the room, and speak with the "pastor," asking for guidance and enlightenment. Time and again, the responses she received were emotionally driven answers and the wrong direction to "pray Jesus into her heart." When the emotional high of praying Jesus into her heart would go away, she would always feel like something was missing. Discouraged each time, she would leave one religious event after another. She then told me that no one had offered to study the Scriptures with her until now. Stunned, yet faith began to surge into my heart, I invited her to lunch and then to our home for a Bible study.

As we walked and talked, I saw a young woman approaching us, and I thought to myself once more: I should probably share my faith and show her an example of how disciples evangelize. Thus, I shared clumsily with the woman that came towards us as my guest looked on. We continued to my house, and there did a Bible study on *Seeking God*.

The Scriptures so inspired the young woman that she begged to continue to study the Bible right then and there. I could not believe what was happening! Despite how obvious God was making it that He was answering my prayer, I was so weak that it was still unclear.

After another hour, we closed the Bible on the last Scripture of the *Word of God Study*. The young woman's hunger to continue to study increased even more. Now I was scared. What was happening? Again, she begged to continue studying the Bible, so we moved on to the *Discipleship Study*.

Initially, she professed to be a disciple, but by the end of the study, the Bible's truth of what it means to follow Jesus became apparent, and she became convinced of where she stood before God. Throughout all the studies, I felt the stiring of the Spirit with every Scripture in my own heart.

Then the young woman looked me in the eye and said something that I will never forget, "I am not leaving here until you baptize me." At that moment, the flame of zeal was reignited in my heart, and I saw the hand of God. I heard His call. He had not forgotten me. He was answering my prayer. He was not done with me, and He replaced my heart of stone with a heart of flesh once more. (Ezekiel 36:26)

So, we continued to study the Bible. Tim came home and was such an incredible encouragement to us, as he dug into our refrigerator, removed a turkey that we had been saving and prepared it for our guest. Even though it was not the October Canadian Thanksgiving, we had a delicious "Thanksgiving meal" together. I am forever grateful for my husband, a true partner in the gospel and a man who has never hesitated to pick me up and carry me in this spiritual race when I am too weak to run on my own. That evening, Tim jumped into our Bible Study when I did not know what to do or what to say.

We partnered together to help this amazing young woman understand the *First Principles Study* called *Light and Darkness*. Nothing is better than working alongside your husband to seek and save the lost. We had been placed into her life, but I also saw how God had placed this woman into my life… saving me from lukewarmness.

That evening, at approximately 11:00 PM, dressed in my t-shirt and shorts, I had the honor to baptize Megan (Bard) Studer in our bathtub as a disciple of Jesus Christ! That night in tears, I thanked God for not giving up on me. The fact that Megan was baptized was only by the power of God. I had been so weak, and there was "no doubt" of that! God used a broken vessel such as myself, even though I had fallen so far. I vowed to do everything that I could to help this young woman stay faithful!

Megan Studer was converted in Toronto in 2006!

Fourteen years later, Megan is a faithful disciple co-leading the Vancouver (Canada) Remnant Group with her awesome husband Jake. Before this, Megan accompanied Tim and me all over the world - on and off the mission field. While we are the same age, in every way she was a loyal and faithful daughter in the faith. God has since blessed Jake and her with three beautiful children.

Doubt in our hearts will threaten to overtake our good confession, and it surely will, if we let it. When this happens, we have a choice. Like Sarah, we can laugh in disbelief, or conversely, we can remember the promises of God. We can go before the Creator of the universe, praying what for us in that moment of doubt may be an impossible prayer, and God will answer it.

As Sarah wanted a child, we want to see more and more sons and daughters come to God through the waters of baptism. If much time has passed since you have participated in baptizing someone, your spiritual barrenness can make you feel "dried up." It is easy to give in to skepticism and doubt. Nevertheless, Jesus commanded "everyone" to *"go and make disciples."* (Matthew 28:19) You can even begin saying to yourself, "Maybe fruitfulness should be a special ministry in our church," or "Maybe I do not have the gift of 'making disciples.'" Of course, as my friend Tony Untalan has said, "When we are doing poorly spiritually, we give in to 'stinking thinking!'" Indeed, time creates the Paper Tiger of Doubt like nothing else. Much like Sarah, we lose patience in God's promise that He wants to make all disciples fruitful. (Matthew 28:19-20)

When I sense the stalking of the Paper Tiger of Doubt, I try to remember the words of Erin Hanson, "What if I fall? …Oh, but my darling, what if you fly?"

"When you relinquish the desire to control your future, you can have more happiness."

Nicole Kidman

Paper Tiger Two
Rebekah's Desire For Control

Rebekah and Eliezer
Bartolomé Esteban Murillo (17th Century)

Abraham was now very old, and the Lord had blessed him in every way. He said to [Eliezer] the senior servant in his household, the one in charge of all that he had, "Put your hand under my thigh. I want you to swear by the Lord, the God of Heaven and the God of Earth, that you will not get a wife for my son from the daughters of the Canaanites, among whom I am living, but will go to my country and my own relatives and get a wife for my son Isaac."
(Genesis 24:1-4)

Abraham charged his servant, likely Eliezer (Genesis 15:2), to return to his people to find a wife for his son. Eliezer did as commanded, and God led him to Rebekah. Rebekah, whose name means "to tie firmly" or "to be captivating," became Isaac's wife and the mother of Esau and Jacob. She was the granddaughter of Nahor, Abraham's brother.[9]

Her family was persuaded that it would be good for her to go. However, *"They said, 'Let's call the young woman and ask her about it.' So they called Rebekah and asked her, 'Will you go with this man?' 'I will go,' she said."* (Genesis 24:57-58)

Arguably, Rebekah is one of the most energetic women in the Bible. The verb "go" is used in concurrence with her at least seven times. She filled up jars with water, cared for livestock, was hospitable, and prepared a place for Abraham's servant and his camels. She ran; she rode a camel; she chose to "go" to be with Isaac. The Bible paints a picture of a dynamic and active woman who is not afraid of adventure.

The Scripture also speaks to the parents and how much they cherished their daughter. They gave her a choice. She was not forced to go, but rather, asked if she would like to go. We gain some insight into why Rebekah was such a confident and secure young woman at that time; her opinion was valued.

---

[9] https://www.chabad.org/library/article_cdo/aid/246617/jewish/Isaacs-Marriage.htm

Upon meeting this incredible, enthusiastic and adventurous Rebekah, *"Isaac brought her into the tent of his mother Sarah, and he married Rebekah. So she became his wife, and he loved her; and Isaac was comforted after his mother's death."* (Genesis 24:67) Rebekah had a boldness about her, which was one of her many strengths. Like Isaac's mother, who followed Abraham wherever the Lord led them, Rebekah was willing to follow Isaac in the same way. Unlike his parents, she was his only wife, a sharp contrast to Abraham, Sarah and Hagar.

Rebekah at the Well
Michael Deas (1995)

Very different than Rebekah, Isaac is depicted as a less dynamic character. While he became immensely wealthy, he gave up his land to the Philistines, who drove him off on several occasions before finding land to settle in Beersheba. (Genesis 26:33)

Isaac was either passive or unwitting in much of the narrative. The sole exception is where he prayed for his barren wife to have children. God listened to Isaac and answered his prayer, allowing Rebekah to become pregnant with twins. God showed his love for Isaac by going above and beyond his request for a child and gave him twins!

> *Isaac prayed to the Lord on behalf of his wife, because she was childless. The Lord answered his prayer, and his wife Rebekah became pregnant. The babies jostled each other within her, and she said, "Why is this happening to me?" So she went to inquire of the Lord.*
>
> *The Lord said to her,*
>
> *"Two nations are in your womb, and two peoples from within you will be separated; one people will be stronger than the other, and the older will serve the younger."* (Genesis 25: 21-23)

It is important to note that Rebekah was a spiritual woman with whom God talked. That being said, she was flawed, as we will soon see. Moreover, she knew God's intention to have Jacob lead Esau; it is not explicitly stated that Isaac knew of this, so we might presume that he did not know.

From this singular conversation, God's view of women is clear: Rebekah, after Eve, Hagar and Sarah, is the fourth woman in the Bible with whom God speaks directly. God desires to have a relationship with women.

The differences between Esau and Jacob could not have been more stark. The Bible refers to Esau as a skilled hunter, someone who would have been more of a "risk-taker" or an adventurer. From the Scriptures, we may surmise that Esau was extroverted in terms of personality and quite passionate. However, he was led by his emotions.

Conversely, Jacob was much quieter. The Bible states that he preferred to stay home among the tents and that he was a calm and simple man. Jacob was undoubtedly the more introverted of the two.

> *The boys grew up, and Esau became a skillful hunter, a man of the open country, while Jacob was content to stay at home among the tents. Isaac, who had a taste for wild game, loved Esau, but Rebekah loved Jacob.* (Genesis 25: 27-28)

From this passage, we learn that while Isaac loved Esau, Rebekah loved Jacob. The family was seemingly divided because Isaac loved wild game and appreciated his eldest son's hunting expertise. However, Rebekah might have remembered God's promise that her younger son would be His people's stronger leader. She became an immense influence in his life.

Esau and Jacob had both strengths and weaknesses: Esau's strength was that he was courageous, daring, and an accomplished hunter. In an article written called *These 5-*

Character Traits Are Found In Every Successful Hunter, the five-character traits are:

> 1) Confidence: Believing that you can do it. 2) Patience: Being willing to wait for the most opportune time to take action. 3) Killer Instinct: A natural timing when it comes to the killer stroke. 4) Detail Oriented: Knowing where to hit in order to bring about an [instant] death. 5) Lucky: Placing yourself in a position to be successful.[10]

The Bible says that Esau was skilled, and so he would have most likely been extremely proficient in these areas. There might have been independence in him as he is called a man of the open country. The *Pulpit Commentary* describes him as "one addicted to roaming through the hills in search of sport."

Conversely, according to the Pulpit Commentary, Jacob is referred to as a man of "mild and gentle manners… preferring a quiet, peaceable, domestic and pious manner of existence."[11]

Seemingly, Esau and Jacob battled for the birthright as they were born. (Genesis 25:22) However, Jacob loses to his brother as Esau's physical strength was apparently superior. After they grew into adults, the birthright was surrendered by Esau to Jacob.

---

[10]https://www.wideopenspaces.com/5-character-traits-found-every-successful-hunter/ by Bill De Gideo
[11]https://biblehub.com/commentaries/genesis/25-27.htm

> *Once when Jacob was cooking some stew, Esau came in from the open country, famished. He said to Jacob, "Quick, let me have some of that red stew! I'm famished!" (That is why he was also called Edom.)*
>
> *Jacob replied, "First sell me your birthright."*
>
> *"Look, I am about to die," Esau said. "What good is the birthright to me?"*
>
> *But Jacob said, "Swear to me first." So he swore an oath to him, selling his birthright to Jacob.*
>
> *Then Jacob gave Esau some bread and some lentil stew. He ate and drank, and then got up and left.*
>
> *So Esau despised his birthright.* (Genesis 25:29-34)

The character flaws in Esau resulted in a grave error. The rights of the firstborn include special privileges and advantages, including the judicial authority of his father. (2 Chronicles 21:3) It was the firstborn son's responsibility to lead the family upon his father's death, honoring his father through his leadership. In addition to that, God would also look favorably upon whoever was chosen and would bless him. This is why Esau's behavior is so disparaged: Knowing the importance of the firstborn role, in a moment of immaturity, he sold his birthright for mere food. We gain an even better insight into the type of character Esau had from the Book of Hebrews:

> *See that no one is sexually immoral, or is godless like Esau, who for a single meal sold his inheritance rights as the oldest son. Afterward, as you know, when he wanted to inherit this blessing, he was rejected. Even though he sought the blessing with tears, he could not change what he had done.* (Hebrews 12:16-17)

Both the Old and New Testaments condemn the actions of Esau, and to this day, he serves as a warning sign for men and women not to be rash. The *Pulpit Commentary* contemplates that Esau sought to regain a blessing but not with a repentant heart.[12]

Rash decisions can result in consequences that continue in others' lives. Esau might have had his mother's resourcefulness and energy as an active hunter, but not her cleverness or her wisdom, like Jacob did. And so, when the time came for Isaac to give his blessing, he made one final request:

> *When Isaac was old and his eyes were so weak that he could no longer see, he called for Esau his older son and said to him, "My son."*
>
> *"Here I am," he answered.*

---

[12]https://biblehub.com/commentaries/pulpit/hebrews/12.htm

> *Isaac said, "I am now an old man and don't know the day of my death. Now then, get your equipment - your quiver and bow - and go out to the open country to hunt some wild game for me. Prepare me the kind of tasty food I like and bring it to me to eat, so that I may give you my blessing before I die."*
>
> *Now Rebekah was listening as Isaac spoke to his son Esau.* (Genesis 27:1-5)

Rebekah was aware that Isaac planned to solidify Esau's leadership and that it was not God's plan. Esau was driven by his flesh; he was at the whim of his emotions. This would not have made him a good leader of his family upon the passing of his father. At this point, the Bible signals a message to us: at an old age, Isaac *"could no longer see."* So for Rebekah, Isaac was physically unable to see and was spiritually unable to see when it comes to his judgment of character regarding his favorite son.

Unfortunately, instead of searching for a godly solution, Rebekah decided to act independently of God and gave direction to Jacob:

> *"Now, my son, listen carefully and do what I tell you: Go out to the flock and bring me two choice young goats, so I can prepare some tasty food for your father, just the way he likes it. Then take it to your father to eat, so that he may give you his blessing before he dies."*

> *Jacob said to Rebekah his mother, "But my brother Esau is a hairy man while I have smooth skin. What if my father touches me? I would appear to be tricking him and would bring down a curse on myself rather than a blessing."*
>
> *His mother said to him, "My son, let the curse fall on me. Just do what I say; go and get them for me."* (Genesis 27:8-13)

In an attempt to control the outcome, Rebekah taught her son to be deceptive towards his father. Her devotion was so complete to her son and the plan that she would take on any possible curse if the plan was discovered. It would seem that the need for control was "learned behavior," as her brother Laban was later equally deceitful with Jacob. Lying and betrayal are considered major sins in the Bible, and although Rebekah is not condemned directly in Scripture, the teachings of the Bible are very clear.

Rebekah wanted to see the will of God happen so desperately that she breaks God's very commandments. Jacob found two goats, and Rebekah prepared them and then helped disguise Jacob as his brother. Isaac was deceived and then blessed Jacob. When he realized this, he tells Esau:

> *When Esau heard his father's words, he burst out with a loud and bitter cry and said to his father, "Bless me - me too, my father!"*

> *But he said, "Your brother came deceitfully and took your blessing."* (Genesis 27:34-35)

It was too late. The blessing could not be reversed. This event caused a severe rift between the brothers, and most likely, between Rebekah and Isaac.

> *Esau held a grudge against Jacob because of the blessing his father had given him. He said to himself, "The days of mourning for my father are near; then I will kill my brother Jacob."* (Genesis 27:41)

No stranger to killing, Esau was able to focus his "killer instinct" on his brother. Esau's character flaw in following his emotions gripped him. He was confident in his ability and patiently waited for his father's mourning period to be over before the murder. He was resolved to take his brother's life with no concern for his mother. He devised his plan and waited for his chance to strike.

> *When Rebekah was told what her older son Esau had said, she sent for her younger son Jacob and said to him, "Your brother Esau is planning to avenge himself by killing you. Now then, my son, do what I say: Flee at once to my brother Laban in Haran. Stay with him for a while until your brother's fury subsides. When your brother is no longer angry with you and forgets what you did to him, I'll send word for you to come back from there. Why should I lose both of you in one day?"* (Genesis 27:42-45)

Once again, Rebekah acted independently of God and sent Jacob to live with her brother Laban until Esau's hatred subsided. Interestingly, Rebekah tells Jacob that she does not want to lose both Jacob and Esau in one day. *The Cambridge Bible for Schools and Colleges Commentary* says, "Or possibly, 'you both' refers to Isaac, her husband, and Jacob, her favorite son. On the day of Isaac's death, Esau intended to slay Jacob."[13]

This would have been too much for a wife and mother to bear. Losing a husband in this period would have been particularly overwhelming. She would have been left without the love of her life, but also her protector. To then lose her beloved son, that God had ordained to be the next leader of the family, would have been catastrophic.

The responsibility for the sad state of this family falls on both Rebekah and Isaac. Rebekah's desire for control and a lack of surrender - coupled with a passive attitude and lack of leadership on Isaac's behalf - destroyed the family's unity. Surprisingly, even though Rebekah fell prey to her "need" for control in this area, overall, she is an exemplary woman in the Scriptures. She was a woman of faith with a deep love for God and a desire to "go!" Rebekah's partiality and upbringing of her son Jacob were otherwise excellent, though most likely her influence on Esau was muted by Isaac's favoritism. She had made such an incredible impact on her son's life that when Jacob first met Rachel, his future wife, he introduced himself as a son of Rebekah and not Isaac! (Genesis 29:12) This observation was noted in rabbinical texts.

---

[13]https://biblehub.com/commentaries/genesis/27-45.htm

As women, we possess an amazing aptitude to influence and change situations around us. We have so many abilities to make situations better when we are full of faith and love God deeply. However, there can be an underlying lack of surrender and desire to control our surroundings hiding deep in our characters that can come up in times of stress or fear. Just as Eve wanted to be *"like God,"* we can want to have total control. (Genesis 3:5) We can then say and do things that we know are wrong to achieve something we believe is right. We can rationalize and convince ourselves of our sinful course of action, and those actions can have lasting consequences in the lives of those we love.

What if Rebekah had prayed? What if she had reasoned with her husband? What if she had poured her heart out to God and trusted that He is sovereign? Remember Abraham and Isaac... At the last moment, God stayed the knife and did not allow Isaac to be killed.

It is essential that we know and obey the following passage, *"All Scripture is God-breathed and is useful for teaching, rebuking, correcting and training in righteousness, so that the servant of God may be thoroughly equipped for every good work."* (2 Timothy 3:16-17)

When I think of the dangers of having an ungodly desire for control, I think of my family's journey to Paris, France in 2012. In 2009, since Tim and I were fluent in French, Kip asked us to begin preparations to plant the Paris Church in 2012. At the time, we were leading the London Remnant Group Church, and it required us to move back to Los

Angeles for more training. After much prayer, we decided to accept the call to train to lead and plant the church in Paris. We believed this was God's calling for our lives.

Upon returning to Los Angeles, we were asked to lead the "sensational" South Region of the City of Angels International Christian Church and begin to assemble our Paris Mission Team. I will never forget the miracles that God allowed us to participate in during our two years of training under the McKeans.

I appreciate our time in Los Angeles as that was when we built friendships with such incredible disciples as Raul and Lynda Moreno, Andrew and Patrique Smellie, Nick and Denise Bordieri, Micheal and Sharon Kirchner, Lance and Connie Underhill, and Jason and Sarah Dimitry. It was also when we witnessed the baptisms of Michelle Miranda, Heidi Santa Cruz, Sean and Eric Valenzuela, Daniela Woody, Bydea Faithful-Bell, Joe Cannon, and Erika and Mercedes Bonilla!

At the 2012 Global Leadership Conference, the Paris Mission Team was sent out by prayer with the expectation of abundant fruit. A week later, we landed in Paris and quickly went to work. In those first 12 weeks, God allowed us to see 13 souls added to our fledgling church! I truly believed that God's plan was for us to be in France for the rest of our lives. I had fully and completely given my heart to Paris and to Europe.

It was such a joy to be in Paris and building a great partnership with Philippe and Prisca Scheidecker - the Paris Remnant Group Leaders. Prisca and I became instant best friends. Like "hand in glove," we worked together so well, and I was extremely excited about the fruitful labor ahead of us.

The Paris Mission Team was sent out at the 2012 Global Leadership Conference!

On the Paris Mission Team, Anthony and Cassidy Olmos - the current leaders of the Paris ICC – became true family with the Author and her husband!

Just as we began to see the fruit of our labor increase, disaster struck. Three months into our stay in the City of Lights, we prepared to return to Canada for Christmas. We were assured that our visas would be delivered to us there. After a week in Canada, we received the news that our visas had been denied. When Tim and I failed to secure our French visas, we were devastated.

**Prisca Scheidecker and the Author
in their beloved Paris!**

The first campus baptism in Paris was Deanna!

For two years, we had prepared ourselves to plant the Paris Church. We had high hopes and prayers for all that God would do. The Paris disciples were awaiting our return. Everything we owned was back in Paris, and we suddenly found ourselves without a home and only the bags that we had with us.

The overwhelming feeling that I experienced was that God had "removed us from the office of leadership." I reflected on what this meant for my family. The feeling of being rejected by the French government and even by God was overwhelming. From Ottawa, where we stayed with my mother and stepfather, we drove to seek refuge at the closest church in our fellowship of churches in Syracuse, New York - overseen by Andrew and Patrique Smellie.

The Smellies and Kernans worked together during our stay in the State of New York.

I will be forever grateful to the Smellies and the disciples in the Syracuse and New York City Churches. They made sure that our children could have a wonderful Christmas despite the circumstances. I am also thankful for disciples like Bob and Mary Thomas and Paul and Amy Ludewig for opening up their homes to us during such a difficult time. During those uncertain days, they were steadfast friends and spiritual family to us.

Tim Junior and David respectively celebrated their third and first Christmases in Syracuse.

We made every effort to be of service to the Syracuse Church. Praise God, He allowed us to help. While we kept busy, the feeling of insecurity - from a lack of being able to control our circumstances - plagued me regularly. "This was not supposed to happen," I would think to myself. Was it not God's plan for us to be in Europe? After all, we speak French, so how is it that we did not receive our visas? Everything felt out of place for me. Where would we go, what would we do? Had not God wanted to use our lives to serve the church? I could not find surrender. I was at peace about the Paris Church, as Kip had flown there to place the Scheideckers in leadership over this young congregation.

I was so defeated that on one occasion, to control my "seemingly" hopeless situation, I began to wonder if God wanted us to go back to Canada and no longer serve in the full-time ministry. The craving for control manifested in me looking at what secular jobs I might be able to secure if God had indeed rejected the path of ministry.

Praise God for a worldwide church family, as so many Christians prayed on our behalf for God to direct our path. As the Bible says in James 5:16, *"The prayer of a righteous person is powerful and effective."* In a few days, God answered those prayers and showed His favor on us, as on New Year's Eve, we were on our way back to Los Angeles. We once more assumed leadership of the South Region and set to work. The joy of being back was heartwarming. Although there was comfort in landing back in Los Angeles, there was uncertainty in my heart of where God would send us long term.

Back in California, we continued to be tested. We were spiritually barren for three months. I believe that God "closed our womb" not out of a lack of love or faith in us, but to help us remember our *"first love."* (Revelation 2:4) We needed to be reminded that our joy, purpose in the ministry, and sense of worth must come from God. No matter the trial, our love for God and the gratitude we have for our salvation must always come first. And so, we surrendered and prayed to the Lord of the harvest, and He answered.

I am so thankful for my husband Tim who always takes such good care of our boys. He enrolled our eldest son in the Atos Brazilian Jiu-Jitsu Academy. Jiu-Jitsu is a "martial art and combat sport system that focuses on grappling and especially ground fighting."[14] One weekend, while attending a children's Jiu-Jitsu competition with Junior, Tim noticed two very energetic parents of a boy and a girl also competing. Compelled by the love of Christ, Tim shared his faith with them both, and they came out to church. (2 Corinthians 5:14) As our friendships grew, we began to study the Bible with them. After a few short weeks, Andrew and Shamika Johnson married and were baptized into Christ! To this day, our children are great friends.

The Johnsons were baptized through the prayers and efforts of the "sensational" South Region in LA!

Tim and I believed that God had brought us back from France in part for this family. What prayers was God answering, not just for them, but for us as well? Had God uprooted us so that we could help the Johnsons be

---

[14]https://en.wikipedia.org/wiki/Brazilian_jiu-jitsu

reconciled to God? What would have happened if we had not surrendered to coming back to Los Angeles? What if we had gone back to Canada? What would have happened to our faith and even our salvation? What would have happened to the Johnsons' opportunity to become disciples and be married in the Kingdom of God?

In 2019, God allowed us to witness another miracle in seeing Andrew and Shamika's son Drew make Jesus Lord of his life and be baptized! As Junior shared in tears how proud he was of his friend's decision to be baptized, I could not help but cry.

The Kernan and Johnson families on the night of the baptism of the Johnsons' son Drew!

Praise God, we saw an entire family brought into His church after such a time of fruitlessness. Through this miracle, God took away the disappointment I felt. There simply was no more room left in my heart for anything but gratitude.

God comforted me in many ways during that time. Especially so, when God brought my beloved Prisca to LA with her awesome husband Philippe and their precious children. To complete my joy, I had the honor of studying the Bible with Rebecca - the Scheideckers' daughter - and watched her parents baptize her in the Pacific Ocean!

Our desire for control will be tested often. In 2016, during the Christmas holidays, I remember waking to Kip's heartbreaking email regarding Prisca. Prisca had battled cancer many times and had won. This time, however, cancer had returned, and she could not overcome it. Tim asked what had happened, and I told him that Prisca had gone on to glory. Then the tears began to flow.

Rebecca's baptism brought Prisca and the Author even closer together!

We reached out to Philippe and decided to fly out immediately after Christmas Day. I am so grateful for Eleanor, Tim's mother, who could be there with the boys while we were away. On the flight, I prepared myself spiritually, mentally and emotionally. I wanted to be able to comfort and help as much as possible. I decided that I would save my mourning for later, but I would control my emotions while in Paris.

It was one of the most challenging trips that I have ever taken. When I knew that I would be speaking at the funeral, I immediately poured out my heart on paper. I found myself disconnecting my emotions just to get through the day. In my effort to control my sadness when we landed in Paris, something happened: I could not reconnect my heart to my words. I started to worry that I would not be able to connect when the time came to share.

As the days passed and we spent time with everyone, there were tears, but not when I looked at what I had written. When we arrived at the viewing, I went from person to person, holding them and comforting them, but not allowing myself to feel anything.

The day of the funeral came, and I was still disconnected from my words. That morning I had prayed for God to help me honor Prisca. I knew that God would want me to connect. As we sat - watching Philippe and Rebecca walk down the aisle - something clicked into place in my heart. We were all gathered to celebrate Prisca's life. As a slideshow played, and as we all looked at the memories that we had shared with our dear sister in Christ, gratitude welled up in my heart. Finally, I was ready to share and surrender control.

While I shared in French, as that is what Prisca would have wanted, the following is what I originally wrote in English that was translated into French by Sandra Laken-Toto:

"Say not in grief that she is no more but say in thankfulness that she was. A death is not the extinguishing of a light, but the putting out of the lamp because the dawn has come." These are Rabindranath Tagore's words, the first non-European to win the Nobel Prize in Literature in 1913.

When I think of who Prisca was when I first met her, the best way to describe her was a woman who wanted to live life to the full. Even though she knew her life could slip away, she insisted on living. I remember one of our last conversations. She was so grateful for the time she had been given.

I too am grateful for the time that I was privileged to know her. While we only knew one another for four years, the depth of our friendship is an honor that I will cherish in my heart all my life. Our time in Paris is one that I will never forget. We often lamented our not having more time together in this great city, your beautiful Paris.

The day I found out about her passing, I was thinking about how best to put into words this loss. After prayer and meditation, I wrote it online to honor her, and I would like very much to share with you what was on my heart.

When a life passes on, it leaves an empty space in the hearts of those who have loved it, but if the life was a good one, the beautiful memories and heartfelt love that was shared remains behind and slowly fills what was once so suddenly left empty.

My dear Prisca, Your leaving has torn a hole in my heart. I remember you, us and everything that God was able to do because of your love, and so little by little, my heart is being filled up once again with gratitude.

I will take all of the love, the courage, the compassion and the passion that you had in this life and hang it around my neck, close to my heart as a reminder of all that you did for the faith of so many.

I will see you again soon... But not yet.

The Author and her husband at Prisca's Celebration of Life Service.

I finally surrendered to God's will that my friend would go to be with Him. It felt so good, and it made me love God and Prisca even more.

There came a day when Tim and I surrendered fully to whatever God's plan was, be it to go back to France or not. I had stopped fighting the "why" in my heart and decided to "let go."

It was around that time that I began a little mantra (if you will) of two fundamental truths that I have tried to live by in my discipleship ever since, "God is always sovereign, and the Bible is always true." What it means to me is very straightforward. No matter what happens in my life, as long as I believe both of those statements, "God is always sovereign, and the Bible is always true," I will be okay. The moment I no longer believe in one or both of those principles, I am in big trouble.

God has put Tim and me through many trials. Losing the dream to lead the Paris Church and learning about Prisca going to glory were two great trials, but there were many more. I knew I needed healing. What I needed healing from was my lack of gratitude. Somewhere along the way, because of the trials, my appreciation had waned. I discovered that I had a false sense of entitlement. I felt entitled to preach in the city that I loved. I felt entitled for Prisca to live longer instead of being grateful that she had lived that long. Paul's heart was so different than mine.

> *I have learned to be content whatever the circumstances. I know what it is to be in need, and I know what it is to have plenty. I have*

> *learned the secret of being content in any and every situation, whether well fed or hungry, whether living in plenty or in want. I can do all this through Him who gives me strength.*
> (Philippians 4:11-13)

I lost sight of the simple joy and contentment that can be had in all circumstances if what you are grateful for is your salvation. Everything - joy, fulfillment and fruit - spring up from a grateful heart. In Paul's words, Jesus is our strength.

The cure for the Paper Tiger of a Desire for Control is gratitude. When we are grateful for what we have and have had, we can let go. The more we focus on God's sovereignty, even in difficult situations, the more room we leave for God to heal us and not be bitter about what we do not possess.

In 2011, *The Huffington Post* published an article by Ocean Robbins called *The Neuroscience of Why Gratitude Makes Us Healthier*. In Robbins' article, he states:

> Another study on gratitude was conducted with adults having congenital and adult-onset neuromuscular disorders (NMDs), with the majority having post-polio syndrome (PPS). Compared to those who were not jotting down their blessings nightly, participants in the gratitude group reported more hours of sleep each night and feeling more refreshed upon awakening. The gratitude group also reported more satisfaction with their lives as a whole, felt more optimism about the upcoming week, and felt considerably

more connected with others than did participants in the control group.

Perhaps most tellingly, the positive changes were markedly noticeable to others. According to the researchers, "Spouses of the participants in the gratitude (group) reported that the participants appeared to have higher subjective well-being than did the spouses of the participants in the control (group)."

There's an old saying that if you've forgotten the language of gratitude, you'll never be on speaking terms with happiness.

It turns out this isn't just a fluffy idea. Several studies have shown depression to be inversely correlated to gratitude. It seems that the more grateful a person is, the less depressed they are. Philip Watkins, a clinical psychologist at Eastern Washington University, found that clinically depressed individuals showed significantly lower gratitude (nearly 50 percent less) than non-depressed controls.[15]

Gratitude and happiness go hand in hand. Disappointment and feeling out of control will drown us even as Christians. If we are conscious of all the good that God has done, and how He is in control, we can let go and surrender.

---

[15] https://www.huffingtonpost.com/ocean-robbins/having-gratitude-_b_1073105.html

Disappointment, fear, exhaustion and the sense that things are chaotic carries with it the potential of depression and an overwhelming desire to seize control, which means rationalizing sin. Consider James 4:7, *"Submit yourselves therefore to God. Resist the Devil, and he will flee from you."* Even if it is purely intellectual at first and you do not "feel it," submit yourself to the Lord and His plan for your life.

The poet John Keats had a tragic life. When he was eight, his father was trampled by a horse. Following, his mother remarried but was not present for him and eventually died of tuberculosis. Keats ultimately suffers the same fate at the very young age of 25, as he also dies of tuberculosis.

John Keats
William Hilton (1822)

Despite all of the suffering that he endured, John Keats insightfully wrote, "Do you not see how necessary a world of pains and troubles is to school an intelligence and make it a soul? A place where the heart must feel and suffer in a thousand diverse ways...." By God taking us to the edge of disaster even as far as death, He brings out the absolute best things in our character.

Even Jesus struggled to surrender control in hardship:

> *And going a little farther, He fell on the ground and prayed that, if it were possible, the hour might pass from Him. And He said, "Abba, Father, all things are possible for you. Remove this cup from me. Yet not what I will, but what you will."* (Mark 14:35-36 ESV)

It is normal to wrestle with the desire to take matters into our own hands. We must go to God as Jesus did, and God will give us the strength to "let go." God will then grant us peace,

> *Rejoice in the Lord always. I will say it again: Rejoice! Let your gentleness be evident to all. The Lord is near. Do not be anxious about anything, but in every situation, by prayer and petition, with thanksgiving, present your requests to God. And the peace of God, which transcends all understanding, will guard your hearts and your minds in Christ Jesus.* (Philippians 4:4-7)

Rejoicing is the language of surrender. God is in control. We should pray honestly about our needs and desires with thanksgiving for what we have. God will protect your mind and your heart in His loving hands. *"Humble yourselves, therefore, under the mighty hand of God so that at the proper time He may exalt you, casting all your anxieties on Him, because He cares for you."* (1 Peter 5:6-10 ESV)

When we are stuck in a desire to gain control of a situation, the worst thing to do is to act or react without first consulting the Scriptures and knowing God's way of doing things. Praying to understand a situation is not the goal. The goal is to pray for a surrendered heart. That is what transcends whether or not you fully comprehend why things are happening the way they are.

The issue was not a lack of understanding. It was a lack of surrender. Rebekah was not at peace with what happened and so she sought to control it. As a result of Isaac's and her actions and inactions, her family was divided.

> *Finally, brothers and sisters, whatever is true, whatever is noble, whatever is right, whatever is pure, whatever is lovely, whatever is admirable - if anything is excellent or praiseworthy - think about such things.* (Philippians 4:8)

As women, it is so vital that we stay positive in our thinking. This is a profound truth: Cynicism and a lack of interest in the good are guaranteed to lead to misery. As the Bible reads, *"For as he thinketh in his heart, so is he."*

(Proverbs 23:7 KJV) You will eventually embody the character traits about which you think. Think about the *"noble, right, pure, lovely, admirable, excellent and praiseworthy..."* and God will be able to bless others through you and you will also be blessed. Focusing on the positive things and keeping a daily record of them will help us avoid dwelling on the negative and foster a healthier outlook whenever we are tempted to give in to negativity. Rebekah was not focused on the godly. The negative drove her to action.

We are what we think, and we will live out whatever we are... to our salvation or to our eternal destruction. Training our hearts and minds to have noble motives will allow us to carry out godly actions. Counter-intuitively, we can only learn this through suffering.

As Christians, the forgiveness of sins - paired with the gift of the Holy Spirit - is proof enough that the Lord has been good to us. Circumstances can change, and most times, we will not be in control. Negativity only breeds negativity.

Rebekah and her family would have greatly benefitted from being surrendered. There is an ease and a lightness that comes from entrusting yourself to God. Christians who clothe themselves with the strength and dignity that comes from putting the Bible into practice do not lose heart when they consider their future. Surrender brings grace, goodness and gratitude to their hearts.

In the words of Steven Hayes, a clinical psychologist at the University of Nevada, "If you always do what you've always done, you'll always get what you've always got."[16] The Paper Tiger of Desire for Control will cause us to repeat the same damaging behavior until we lose ourselves. God, however, wishes for us to break out of our restraints and be free.

Let go and let God mold you into the woman you are meant to be.

---

[16]https://www.psychologytoday.com/us/blog/in-practice/201301/anxiety-quotes-the-ten-best-quotes-about-overcoming-anxiety-0

"Insecurity is at the heart of every rivalry."

Beth Moore

Paper Tiger Three
Rachel's Rivalry

Vision of Rachel and Leah
Dante Gabriel Rossetti (1855)

When the Lord saw that Leah was not loved, He enabled her to conceive, but Rachel remained childless. Leah became pregnant and gave birth to a son. She named him Reuben, for she said, "It is because the Lord has seen my misery. Surely my husband will love me now." She conceived again, and when she gave birth to a son she said, "Because the Lord heard that I am not loved, He gave me this one too." So she named him Simeon.

Again she conceived, and when she gave birth to a son she said, "Now at last my husband will become attached to me, because I have borne him three sons." So he was named Levi.

She conceived again, and when she gave birth to a son she said, "This time I will praise the Lord." So she named him Judah. Then she stopped having children.

When Rachel saw that she was not bearing Jacob any children, she became jealous of her sister. So she said to Jacob, "Give me children, or I'll die!" (Genesis 29:31-30:1)

Similar to his grandfather Abraham, Jacob married two women. The history of polygamy stretches back to Genesis 4, where Lamech, a descendant of Cain, is the first recorded example of having two wives.[17] According to the *Jewish Encyclopedia*, the practice of polygamy was commonplace during Jacob's lifetime due to the influence of the Canaanites.

---

[17] https://amazingbibletimeline.com/blog/lamech-first-polygamist/

As Abraham did with Isaac, Rebekah counseled her son Jacob against marrying a Canaanite woman and sent him to her people to find a wife. (Genesis 27:46) It is there that Jacob first encountered the beautiful Rachel and worked seven years for her father, his uncle Laban. While he desired to marry Rachel, Jacob was tricked by Laban into marrying his eldest daughter, Leah. Out of love for Rachel, Jacob agreed to work for his uncle another seven years to marry her as well.

These two women suffer from two different types of barrenness. While Rachel was devoid of the ability to bear offspring, Leah was devoid of the love of her husband. Rachel enjoyed the fruits of her husband's love, and Leah enjoyed the fruits of bearing children, so each was not content. (Genesis 29:30)

Due to her inability to have children, in contrast to her sister Leah's fruitfulness, Rachel's frustration with her situation manifested itself through deep resentfulness and competition with her sister. Her solution to her predicament was to offer her maidservant to her husband and make a family through her. History heartbreakingly repeats itself as Rachel follows in the steps of her "grandmother-in-law" - Sarah.

> *Jacob became angry with her and said, "Am I in the place of God, who has kept you from having children?"*
>
> *Then she said, "Here is Bilhah, my servant. Sleep with her so that she can bear children for me and I too can build a family through her."*

> *So she gave him her servant Bilhah as a wife. Jacob slept with her, and she became pregnant and bore him a son. Then Rachel said, "God has vindicated me; He has listened to my plea and given me a son." Because of this she named him Dan.*
>
> *Rachel's servant Bilhah conceived again and bore Jacob a second son. Then Rachel said, "I have had a great struggle with my sister, and I have won." So she named him Naphtali.*
> (Genesis 30:2-8)

Rachel was deceived. In her mind, she convinced herself that the children her maidservant was bearing would heal her of her jealousy. Though legally, the children would have been counted as her own, Bilhah's relationship with them would always create a problem. Like Sarah, the only thing that Rachel was doing in giving her maidservant to her husband was creating more potential for the rivalry to thrive. If only she knew what the consequences of her actions would produce later.

When couples wrestle with infertility, it can strain the relationship to the point that it can be difficult to overcome. An article written in *The Atlantic* about infertility and marriage provides a striking similarity to Rachel and Jacob's exchange. One reader writes:

> I'm 36 and I've been struggling with infertility for a bit over a year now. I say "I" because from my point of view, this is much more my problem than

my husband's. (Yes, he's had tests done and all is normal.) I know many men are as heartbroken as their partners over trying to conceive, but that hasn't been my experience, nor my friends'. My husband loves me and wants me to be happy, but it's very simple for him to say "we'll adopt" or "we'll have a baby some way; you'll be a mother." It's very different to be the one who feels that her body doesn't work; who doesn't feel like a woman; who feels as if life is passing her by every day that passes without a baby.

I feel guilt and anger every day about waiting so long to try to get pregnant; anger at my husband for persuading me to wait until we were 35 to start trying; anger at myself for listening to him when having a family is my life's goal.

I also struggle with jealousy. "Oh! We weren't even trying to get pregnant!" Even a good friend of mine at age 42 is about to have a baby girl via IVF. I think of her every day and hope I am so lucky.[18]

The effects of a ***"hope deferred"*** can bring about a fit of anger, frustration and even, in the case of Rachel, blame-shifting. (Proverbs 13:12) Rachel lashed out at Jacob and blamed him for her inability to bear children. Jacob was not in a good place spiritually and gave full vent to his anger. Sadly, during this fight, Rachel offered her maidservant to

---

[18] https://www.theatlantic.com/notes/2016/10/when-infertility-threatens-marriage/505436/

Jacob out of sheer desperation, and in an attempt to please her, Jacob agreed.

What eventually transpired was a strange rivalry between Rachel and Leah for who will have more children. They were the victims of a "love triangle" orchestrated by their father Laban. Leah would have known that the marriage had been built on a lie, as she was complicit in deceiving Jacob.

Leah's insecurity would have been there from the very beginning of her marriage to Jacob. After all, Leah watched her husband get married to her little sister Rachel just a week after Leah's wedding. (Genesis 29:28) Then Leah watched her husband work seven more years in an agreement between Jacob and her father for Rachel's hand. It surely would have put a deep resentment in her heart toward Rachel. This created a rivalry between the two sisters. Marriage is a sacred relationship and there is nothing worse than an unloved woman. Consequently, she thought that having several children with Jacob would win his heart.

Rachel, on the other hand, failed to appreciate the pain of her older sister. She was blind to the fact that Leah was barren of love and desperate for affection. Rachel was loved from the very day that she met Jacob. Rachel was valued not for the children she could have but for who she was.

What a sad and tragic account. One woman was the recipient of conditional love through childbearing; the other woman seeking purpose in childbearing while receiving unconditional love. Each wanted so desperately what the other had. This caused heartache for so many. The rivalry became so dark that each woman allowed the exchanging "goods" for the privilege of spending the night with their shared husband. In Hebrew literature, the goods bartered were mandrakes - thought to be a cure for sterility and an aphrodisiac.

> *In the days of wheat harvest Reuben went and found mandrakes in the field and brought them to his mother Leah. Then Rachel said to Leah, "Please give me some of your son's mandrakes." But she said to her, "Is it a small matter that you have taken away my husband? Would you take away my son's mandrakes also?" Rachel said, "Then he may lie with you tonight in exchange for your son's mandrakes." When Jacob came from the field in the evening, Leah went out to meet him and said, "You must come in to me, for I have hired you with my son's mandrakes." So he lay with her that night."* (Genesis 30:14-16 ESV)

The family dynamic was full of so much pain and so much anger. Leah blames Rachel for "taking her husband," even though their father Laban was the catalyst.

Astonishingly, God finally grants Rachel the desire of her heart and allows her to give birth to Joseph. While it may seem unclear as to why God would wait for so long, we look at the delayed births - of Isaac, Jacob and now Joseph - and we see they had a particular purpose in the plans of God.

> *Then God remembered Rachel; He listened to her and enabled her to conceive. She became pregnant and gave birth to a son and said,*

"God has taken away my disgrace." She named him Joseph, and said, "May the Lord add to me another son." (Genesis 30:22-24)

The phrase - "God remembered" - may cause confusion in the reader. Is that to mean that God "forgets?" *Elliot's Commentary for English Readers* says, "Rachel's long barrenness had probably humbled and disciplined her; and, cured of her former petulance, she trusted no longer in "love-apples" [meaning mandrakes] but looked to God for the great blessing of children. He hearkened to her prayers and remembered her."[19]

When the rivalry came to an end, the disgrace departed. The Bible says, **"God remembered her."** It is here that Rachel, according to the *Pulpit Commentary,* "was able to recognize her complete dependence for offspring on the sovereign grace of the covenant of God [with] Abraham and Isaac and Jacob."[20] What a powerful moment.

When the sisters finally end their rivalry, the disgrace was alleviated for Rachel, and conditional love was alleviated for Leah. This is not to say that their interactions were what God desired, of course. The conclusion to their rivalry was to make their way back to God.

Rachel learned it was not a maidservant or mandrakes that would **"enable her to conceive,"** but reliance on God. She

---

[19] https://biblehub.com/genesis/30-22.htm
[20] http://Biblehub.com/genesis/30-22.htm

then asked God for one more son. In Genesis 35, God answered her prayers, sadly at the cost of her life.

> *Then they moved on from Bethel. While they were still some distance from Ephrath, Rachel began to give birth and had great difficulty. And as she was having great difficulty in childbirth, the midwife said to her, 'Don't despair, for you have another son.' As she breathed her last - for she was dying - she named her son Ben-Oni. But his father named him Benjamin.* (Genesis 35:16-18)

God gave Rachel the son for which she prayed, but ironically, this brought to fruition the ultimatum that she had given earlier to her husband, **"Give me children, or I'll die."** After her second son Benjamin was born, the Bible says that Rachel breathed her last. (Genesis 30:1)

For most of my Christian walk, I have felt like God has given me the desires of my heart. I prayed specifically for certain things that I was looking for in a husband, and I believe that God answered every one of them. I am very grateful that my husband and I have one another in this life. Tim is my best friend.

During our early years of marriage, Tim and I had always been members of or led small churches. The close relationships that one can share with other Christians in a small group setting became some of the best memories that I had in the ministry. For me, getting to serve God and "blend into the background" was my ideal. When I had a backyard for my kids to run around in and a small ministry to grow, I was content.

In the ministry, however, God has tested my faith on many occasions. While I am not a very competitive person by nature, I have seen the damage that ungodly competition born of jealousy and envy can wreak.

In 2014, about seven months into leading the Toronto International Christian Church, Tim received a call from Kip. Flabbergasted, Tim agreed to speak to me about it. So, after much prayer and advice, we agreed to leave Toronto and return to Los Angeles to prepare to lead the largest church in the Movement of almost 1,000 disciples – the City of Angels International Christian Church.

When Tim told me about this new opportunity, anxiety flooded my heart. Who were we to lead a church of such magnitude? Satan used my anxiety to convince me that we could never do such a thing. I began to think of every reason why we were not the ones to do it and that there were far more experienced people who would do a better job. As that peaceful heart that I had in Toronto gave way to great apprehension, other negative qualities began to "take residence."

After our return to Los Angeles, at one of the very first LA Staff Meetings that I attended, a Women's Ministry Leader came up to me while I was getting coffee and jokingly said, "So you're the big dog now, huh?" I laughed nervously out of embarrassment and said, "No, no, I'm not…" and wandered off, but I was so disturbed by that interaction. I certainly had not seen myself in that light, and the idea that others may think that I did bothered me immensely. As the saying goes: "One day you're top dog, the next day you're dog meat." I did not want to be either, but the interaction at staff put a strange feeling inside of me that I had not known.

Even though I had nothing to prove as one chosen by God who prepares our works in advance for us to do, I found myself feeling inadequate. (Ephesians 2:10) I thought to myself that I needed to be more extroverted like this sister or more emotionally in touch like that sister, and because I was neither of those things, I became defensive in my heart to protect myself. Defensiveness is a gateway to much more sin, and that was what happened to me. I became defensive, which would come out in my tone and body language, particularly with Tim. My words began to take on an edge. I became argumentative with those around me.

I began to covet my privacy more and more and wanted to get out from under the microscope of people's expectations. The challenges of the "fish-bowl life" were the hardest for me to overcome. The dream of having a "normal life" and staying "under the radar" was no longer possible in Los Angeles. I started getting tempted to "check out" often in meetings and began to attempt to deal with my anxiety through disassociating, staying up late, and oversleeping, trying to fill my troubled heart with food or entertainment. Once I let the discouragements of rivalry into my heart - the constant need to gain self-worth from performance - this was enough to cause me to doubt my calling from God… and in my very darkest moments, even to consider quitting the ministry.

The effects of rivalry were, for me, the single most difficult aspect of leadership. Good-hearted disciples enter into leadership because of their love for God, His great people and the lost. However, as time goes on and sinful natures collide, Satan looks for the weak and weary in leadership to pry apart the church. Eventually, enough unhealed hurt, unrepentant sin, and unresolved anger will build up and create *"a root of bitterness that defiles many."* (Hebrews 12:14-15) In time, I realized something profound: I did not want to suffer. I did not want hardship.

What happens when the women pull back their hearts from one another in the church? What will be the church's fate if the women inside of it are overcome by long-term bitterness and resentment? What will become of our children if their mothers allow themselves to grow weary and lose heart? As women who can struggle with rivalry, we must not flee from it, but instead, we must repent of it. We must also call others to repent of it, learning to work together as a sisterhood. This was my heart when Tim and I assumed the City of Angels Church's leadership on December 13, 2015!

The Author and her husband with Kip and Elena on the day they assumed the leadership of the City of Angels Church.

That next week, we had a retreat to bring the staff together. On Friday night, all the super region leaders met and shared their life stories. It was so encouraging and bonding to hear the fantastic spiritual journey of each leader.

The next night, all the region leaders, shepherds and admins arrived, and we had a delicious dinner. We then had a tearful time of confession split by men and women. Before the confession time, you could feel the tension in the room. Yet as each leader "got open" and confessed their sins and shortcomings, we all endeared ourselves to one another, and any rivalries turned into sibling love.

CAICC Super Region Leaders Retreat. From left to right by couple: Coltin and Mandee Rohn, Blaise and Patricia Feumba, Ron and Tracy Harding, Tim and the Author, Mike and Brittany Underhill, and Ricky and Coleen Challinor.

Thank God for the clarity that comes from confessing your sin. I expressed the need to work together as a team, not competing against one another but working as one sisterhood. It was so unifying. Where Satan wants us to be isolated from one another and live as rivals, God desires us to be close, humble to one another.

After that retreat, something shifted within me. I saw that my lack of openness and transparency had hurt my friendships and, more importantly, my relationship with God. I had pulled my heart back because deep down inside, I felt like God had pulled back His heart from me. Of course, God had not. He bestowed upon me the great honor and privilege of allowing me to suffer in a little way like Christ.

No one loves Jesus more than God the Father, yet He allowed Jesus to suffer terribly at the hands of others. He allowed Jesus to be immersed in toxic environments and "rivalries." God allowed Jesus to go off to solitary places to pray where He would cry out loudly in tears. He did this so that Jesus would be our example when we encounter hardships:

> *For it is commendable if someone bears up under the pain of unjust suffering because they are conscious of God. But how is it to your credit if you receive a beating for doing wrong and endure it? But if you suffer for doing good and you endure it, this is commendable before God. To this you were called, because Christ suffered for you, leaving you an example, that you should follow in His steps. "He committed no sin, and no deceit was found in His mouth."*

> *When they hurled their insults at Him, He did not retaliate; when He suffered, He made no threats. Instead, He entrusted Himself to Him who judges justly. "He Himself bore our sins" in His body on the cross, so that we might die to sins and live for righteousness; "by His wounds you have been healed." For "you were like sheep going astray," but now you have returned to the Shepherd and Overseer of your souls.* (1 Peter 2:19-25)

This Scripture gave a "hard reset" to my perspective. God is more concerned with our eternal contentment rather than our Earthly contentment. We cannot allow what we receive or do not receive to dictate our perception of the level of love God has for us. We cannot find our self-worth and security in things, situations or people. We must find it in entrusting ourselves to God and helping others do the same through counsel and the example we provide. After this great epiphany, I turned my attention to thinking about how I could help others not see "problems" but the "opportunities" of ministry.

Tim began to gather some of the men every Saturday that had a dream for the ministry to train them. As an equal partner in the gospel to my husband, I decided to do the same with the women. This was necessary as the City of Angels Church sends out many mission teams with exceptional leaders, interns and disciples.

Tim called his group the Armor Bearers, and I called my group the Shieldmaidens. We would meet on Saturdays monthly, and I would put together lessons on leadership and the heart we should have if we desire to serve God in the ministry. The first time we met, I centered the study on counting the cost of going into the full-time ministry. It was entitled, *Can You Drink The Cup?* from the First Portland Missions Jubilee. Since I received so much positive feedback, I decided to deliver a short lesson at each meeting. Also, I would give them an article on leadership to read.

One of Tim's and my reasons for having a fellowship for the interns was to imitate the ministry of Jesus. Jesus had His "70" (Luke 10:1), His "12" (Luke 6:12-16), and His "3" (Luke 8:51). Jesus' motives were to focus on the few to benefit the many. So this was the beginning of building Tim's and my "70."

The first official City of Angels Shieldmaidens with the Author in 2016.

The spirit that Tim and I strove to put into the interns was to be followers of Jesus and ***"fishers of men."*** (Matthew

4:19) We taught them the nobility and humility of Jesus that they would need to thrive in ministry. We taught them to find their self-worth not from their performance but from God. There would be no sinful competition between them. Tim would often say, "You are not an Armor Bearer or Shieldmaiden because you are 'awesome.' Every disciple is awesome. You are here because you want to follow Jesus, preach the Word to a lost world, and lay down your life to serve other disciples as leaders." (John 15:13)

In 2017, the Shieldmaidens had multiplied in number in just one year!

What followed was one of the most memorable times in all of my years in the ministry. As the interns grew up together, trained together, were fruitful together, and celebrated special moments together, the City of Angels Church saw many young men and women be prepared to lead. Fast forward to today, and many have gone on to lead powerful regions, super regions and churches, others have become dynamic shepherdesses and administrators. We strove to put to death any rivalry and lift up one another, and the result was beautiful partnerships in the gospel.

In families and businesses today, there are so many evil leadership practices that hurt women. So many are afraid to be "teacher's pets" or "scapegoats" because of past experiences in the world. This is what women often mean when they say they are "not interested in leadership."

Being a leader at any level should never be reduced to a *"Glengarry Glen Ross* sales floor." This movie is a perfect example of how a leadership team should not look. (I cannot recommend this movie as there is foul language in the dialogue.) The movie *Glengarry Glen Ross* "...serves as a microcosm of capitalist culture: As the top man gets a Cadillac and the bottom man gets fired, every man must not only work for his success but also hope for - or actively engineer - his coworkers' failure."[21]

While these godless and uninspiring leadership tactics are ubiquitous in the world - and probably do squeeze a little more productivity out of employees - the toxicity this creates in a church family atmosphere is entirely unacceptable. In the world, people move on to another job. Even in the Kingdom, disciples move from a "sick church" seeking a warm, loving and wholesome environment in another congregation. This explains another reason why churches do not grow.

---

[21]https://www.sparknotes.com/drama/glengarry/themes/

The *Glengarry Glen Ross* Model cannot reflect our interactions at any leadership level in God's Kingdom. The women in the church are co-guardians with the men of the spiritual health of each church family. In our role as women, we must gently and humbly voice our concerns to our husbands, and if appropriate, to our church leaders directly.

Like Rachel, God "remembered me," and I was able to witness many of the Shieldmaidens be appointed to be Women's Ministry Leaders and go on to do great things. Watching young women work together without rivalry for the glory of God is one of the greatest joys of my life. Let me reiterate: Hate rivalry; teach against rivalry; but never run from rivalry. Get comfortable wading into toxicity and creating purity of motivations among the sisters. Let us be the women that God knows we can be. ***"Fix your eyes on Jesus,"*** and work with your fellow sisters in Christ to achieve God's dreams and goals… together. (Hebrews 12:2)

The Shieldmaidens Of The Cross Gallery

Lizbeth Cohen was appointed a Women's Ministry Leader in 2017 when her husband Caleb was appointed an Evangelist!

Karen Gregory was appointed Women's Ministry Leader in 2019!

God blessed Shauna Inkley to be recognized as a Women's Ministry Leader in 2017!

The Esparzas and Grangers were appointed Evangelists and Women's Ministry Leaders in 2020!

The momentous appointments of Lynette Ybarra and Maraia Lastra was in 2020!

Mason and Nathalie Fetelika were appointed Evangelist and Women's Ministry Leader in 2017!

Sean and Krystal O'Connor were appointed
Evangelist and Women's Ministry Leader
in 2018, and then later, they were sent
off to lead the Guam ICC!

The Author, Therese and dear Shieldmaidens from
left to right: Nicole, Devon, Lizbeth, Haley
and Kierra on Heidi's wedding day!

Mialynn became a great young Shieldmaiden and a wonderful addition to the Kernan Clan in 2020!

The Author and Alicia Causey at her appointment by Patricia Feumba as a Women's Ministry Leader in 2020!

Steve and Nancy Stancil lead the IE Vine Sector!

Rico and Janelle Jones serve as the Honolulu Campus Ministry Couple!

The appointment of the Schafers by the Hardings in 2021 was on the mission field of Atlanta!

The appointment of Josiah and Kristin Smith by the Bakers (left) and Zepedas in 2021!

The Kernans celebrated with Michael and Jasmin Peterson at their appointment as Evangelist and Women's Ministry Leader!

Jessie Rojo Kley and the Author at her appointment as Women's Ministry Leader in 2021!

"That feeling of freedom - open highways of possibilities - has been lost to materialism and marketing."

Sheryl Crow

Paper Tiger Four
Lot's Wife's Longing For The World

The Destruction of Sodom and Gomorrah
John Martin (1852)

The story of Lot's wife begins with Lot. His uncle Abraham suggested that Lot and he separate because of the conflict that had arisen between their herdsman. Abraham also thought it would be advantageous due to the size of their families and flocks. (Genesis 13:8-9) Choosing the Jordan's lush plain towards Zoar, Lot set out and eventually settled near the twin cities of Sodom and Gomorrah.

One evening, as Lot was sitting at the city gate, the two angels, who, unbeknownst to him, had just come from the house of his uncle Abraham, approach the city:

> *"My Lords," [Lot] said, "please turn aside to your servant's house. You can wash your feet*

> and spend the night and then go on your way early in the morning."
>
> "No," they answered, "we will spend the night in the square."
>
> But he insisted so strongly that they did go with him and entered his house. He prepared a meal for them, baking bread without yeast, and they ate. Before they had gone to bed, all the men from every part of the city of Sodom - both young and old - surrounded the house. They called to Lot, "Where are the men who came to you tonight? Bring them out to us so that we can have sex with them." (Genesis 19:2-5)

Lot was very concerned about the men wanting to spend the night in the open city square, so he invited them to his house. Interestingly, hospitality is a sign in the Scriptures of righteousness, and Lot is shown to have still been a hospitable man even though he lived in the sinful city of Sodom. An article from Baylor University helps us understand the importance of hospitality in ancient times:

> To fully appreciate this tapestry of stories, we must see them in light of the ancient Mediterranean practice of hospitality and the role it plays in the larger Biblical narrative.
>
> The practice of welcoming travelers emerged in antiquity to "neutralize potential threats - both threats to strangers and threats to one's community," writes Andrew Arterbury. The host

protected a traveler from abuse by fearful townspeople and won the traveler's goodwill for the town. "If they both agreed, a host and guest might exchange valuable gifts that symbolized the formation of a long-term, reciprocal guest-friendship or alliance between the two of them and their families."

Why would anyone extend hospitality to a complete stranger, since it was so risky? A Greco-Roman host might welcome a traveler to avoid offending Zeus, the patron of hospitality, or to establish a strategic alliance. But in a Hebraic or Christian context, "A follower of God showed love for God and others by extending hospitality to complete strangers. In addition, though it was not the primary motivation, some followers of God likely were motivated to extend hospitality to strangers by their desire to cultivate God's blessings upon their own lives and households."

Hospitality is central in the Biblical narrative. The Church is "the household of God," inviting us to dwell with God. (Ephesians 2:19-20; 1 Timothy 3:15; 1 Peter 4:17) The instruction in Hebrews 13:1-2, "Let mutual love continue. Do not neglect to show hospitality to strangers, for by doing that some have entertained angels without knowing it," echoes the stories of Abraham's and Lot's welcoming strangers who were actually Yahweh or Yahweh's angels. (Genesis 18:1-16, 19:1-23)[22]

Similar to Abraham, Lot reached out and offered hospitality to the two angels. As soon as the angels had eaten, the men of the city approached Lot's home. The word had gone out that the newcomers were staying with Lot. The Jewish historian Josephus supposes that these angels "caused a stir among the men of the city due to their handsomeness."[23] As a result, the men of the town converged on Lot's house to have sex with them.

According to the Bible, homosexuality was prevalent among the Canaanites. (Leviticus 18:22-24) All sex outside of marriage is immoral and sexual relations between members of the same sex are prohibited in the Scriptures. (Leviticus 18:22, 1 Timothy 1:10) Appallingly, Lot pleaded with the men by offering his daughters as a way to appease them. (Genesis 19:8) Lot was perceived as a "judgmental" man because he disagreed with what the men wished to do. (Genesis 19:9) The angels interceded at that point by blinding the men at Lot's door and then pulled Lot back into the house, shutting the door behind them.

Lot's offer of his daughters was an uncomfortable example of panic under great distress. Ancient hospitality dictated the pledge of protection of one's guests at all cost. However, the solution Lot offered is horrific. This Scripture is indeed

---

[22]https://www.baylor.edu/content/services/document.php/53391.pdf
[23]http://Biblehub.com/genesis/19-5.htm

difficult to understand, yet an article posted on how anxiety can lead to unethical behavior says the following:

> Anxiety is bad for good behavior. That's because people who feel anxious are more likely to act unethically, according to research by Sreedhari Desai of the University of North Carolina Kenan-Flagler Business School and Maryam Kouchaki of the Kellogg School of Management at Northwestern University.
>
> "Individuals who feel anxious and threatened can take on self-defensive behaviors and focus narrowly on their own basic needs and self-interest," said Desai. "This can cause them to be less mindful of principles that guide ethical and moral reasoning - and make them rationalize their own actions as acceptable."[24]

The angels then urged Lot to warn anyone in his family to escape the city. Sadly, Lot's two sons-in-law, who were pledged to be married to his daughters, thought he was joking. Lot continued to hesitate until the angels forcefully dragged his wife, their two daughters and him out of the city. They urged him to go to the mountains, but Lot insisted on going only as far as the town of Zoar, which means "small." (Genesis 19:12-17) Lot is portrayed as someone who was not taken seriously, who hesitated, had little spiritual strength only to accomplish "small feats," and without realizing it had become warped by the city. All the

---

[24]https://www.kenan-flagler.unc.edu/news/anxiety-can-lead-to-unethical-behavior/

same, Peter helps us to understand how God, who judges the heart, saw Lot:

> *...if (the Lord) condemned the cities of Sodom and Gomorrah by burning them to ashes, and made them an example of what is going to happen to the ungodly; and if He rescued Lot, a righteous man, who was distressed by the depraved conduct of the lawless (for that righteous man, living among them day after day, was tormented in his righteous soul by the lawless deeds he saw and heard) - if this is so, then the Lord knows how to rescue the godly from trials and to hold the unrighteous for punishment on the day of judgment. This is especially true of those who follow the corrupt desire of the flesh and despise authority.* (2 Peter 2:6-10)

This passage should offer us great comfort that God in His grace considered Lot righteous despite so many shortcomings and wrong decisions. However, God does draw a line and makes a judgment between the righteous and the unrighteous. Until this point, Lot's wife was an invisible character in this alarming account. However, now she becomes the grim focus of the story.

> *By the time Lot reached Zoar, the sun had risen over the land. Then the Lord rained down burning sulfur on Sodom and Gomorrah - from the Lord out of the Heavens. Thus He overthrew those cities and the entire plain, destroying all those living in the cities - and*

also the vegetation in the land. But Lot's wife looked back, and she became a pillar of salt. (Genesis 19:23-26)

Lot's wife deliberately disregarded the direction of the angels and brazenly turned back to look. The angels had been very forthright in commanding the family not to do so. Contempt for the angels' instruction resulted in her severe punishment... death.

After departing from Abraham's company, Lot led a life of compromise so much that he eventually moved into the city of Sodom. (Genesis 19:1) Since this was his character, Lot tried to compromise with the angels about how far his family should go from Sodom. The angels did give in to his request. So, it is not surprising that Lot's wife followed her husband's example of compromise with a very different result. She went a step further and disobeyed - thus, she became a pillar of salt.

If we only look at the Old Testament text, it is difficult to understand why Lot's wife turned back. However, Jesus sheds light on this:

It was the same in the days of Lot. People were eating and drinking, buying and selling, planting and building. But the day Lot left Sodom, fire and sulfur rained down from Heaven and destroyed them all. It will be just like this on the day the Son of Man is revealed. On that day no one who is on the housetop, with possessions inside, should go down to get them. Likewise, no one in the field should go back for anything. Remember Lot's wife! Whoever tries to keep their life will lose it, and whoever loses their life will preserve it. (Luke 17:28-33)

According to Jesus, it would seem that Lot's wife turned back to retrieve or at least yearned for her possessions. Lot's wife becomes a warning sign for all of us as we leave our old lives and *"seek first the Kingdom of God."* (Matthew 6:33 ESV) She could not imagine life without her "things." To salvage her old material life, she ended up losing not only all of her material possessions, but she also lost her physical life and… her spiritual life.

Lot and His Family Flee from Sodom
Julius Schnorr von Carolsfeld (1852-60)

The examples of Lot and his wife ended up drastically affecting their daughters. While escaping the fiery demise of

Sodom, Lot later became a victim of incest, having been inebriated by his daughters to preserve the family line. From what we can glean from the Scriptures, Lot was a righteous man, troubled with the sin of Sodom and Gomorrah. He was seemingly unable to affect any change in the city, as he should not have been there in the first place.

The Scriptures seek to paint a clearer picture of Lot's wife and the two daughters. They were quite possibly accustomed to not being protected. So, they began taking matters into their own hands and had become quite independent. The angels attempted to give Lot's wife direction, but it would seem that operating as part of a team was foreign to her, and she ignored them to her destruction.

Lot's daughters eventually find themselves living in a cave with their father. Now away from all other humans, they lack faith because they do not "see God" and thus do not see any potential husbands. They also lack faith in their father's ability to secure their future. Once again, these two women act independently. Tragically, Lot's daughters get their father drunk to be impregnated by him. This decision brings about the Moabite and Ammonite nations, who became the enemies of the Israelites - God's people. (Genesis 19:36-38)

As we read this account, it is very easy to condemn Lot for his lack of leadership. It is effortless to look down on Lot's wife for her poor judgment and very easy to look at Lot's daughters as the worst of women. However, the inconvenient truth is that there is a little bit of Lot, Lot's wife and Lot's daughters in all of us.

Growing up, I loved God. I was raised "Catholic," and my mother would regularly take us to church throughout my childhood. My favorite part was communion. Unfortunately, not because I fully comprehended what communion symbolized, but because I liked the way the circular wafer dissolved in my mouth. After having the wafer placed on my tongue, I would transfer it to the roof of my mouth and then peel it off with my tongue. For a young girl, sitting in church was not the most exciting of activities, and so communion made the remainder of the service more bearable.

During this time, I remember embarrassing my mom one time after church when we thanked the priest for the service. I asked him if he was God. My mom quickly ushered me away, laughing nervously, but I did not know any better. In my mind, I was genuinely perplexed.

The Author and her childhood best friend Josh on the day of her first communion.

As I grew older, I became more and more caught up in the world and began to live a double life. On the one hand, I was the shy, quiet young woman who did not give my mother much reason to worry, but there was another side of me that had begun to experiment with sin.

The "rush" that you get from sin is addictive. At the time, I could not believe how easy it was. While sin had been a shot of adrenaline at the moment, it was always followed by the crash of shame. The cycle began: My sin gradually increased in wickedness as it would take more and more to feel the same rush. (Romans 6:17)

To no surprise, this produced in me an aversion to God to some degree. I have always been a guilty soul, so anything having to do with the Bible or God made me feel shame. After a while, I started dating a young man for the very first time. While God saved me from outright sexual immorality, enough happened with him to give me my share of emotional scars.

Ultimately, I wanted to do what I wanted to do, regardless of the close calls and the warnings. Frequently when you are young and invincible in your own eyes, it sometimes takes extreme heartaches and emotional pain to learn the important lessons of life. This is God's way as He uses hardships - most of whom we bring upon ourselves - to teach us. (Hebrews 12:7)

The world was pulling me in deeper and deeper. At 18, I ended up dating a man six years my senior. I even chose to accept a scholarship at Chicago State University to move to Chicago to be with him. However, God orchestrated events so that I would be back in Canada a month later to solidify my scholarship, so I decided to visit my family in Montreal.

The Author (second row, third on the right) with her track and field club - the Ottawa Lions - in Florida during training.

While living in Montreal, my dad and my stepmother were baptized as disciples in the Toronto International Church of Christ on April 6, 1990. I was just a preteen, but it changed all of our lives. My sister and I would visit every summer, so we would also visit "their church." I will never forget the impact that the Children's Ministry had on me, even as an 11-year-old. The way the disciples poured their time and talents into "us kids" was so incredible. I found myself looking forward to going to church when we would visit. As a result, my older sister Tamara became a baptized disciple at 16 and seeing her change impacted me all the more.

My dad was born and raised in Hamilton, Ontario, about an hour's drive from Toronto, Canada. He is ethnically descended from an African American run-away slave seeking freedom in Canada and the Mohawk chief Joseph

Brant. He was one of the first black professional engineers in Canada. My dad is an amazing man. I remember so clearly the stark contrast between my dad before and after his baptism.

I am so grateful that my father, stepmother and sister decided to become disciples when they did. It allowed me to see the Kingdom of God at a young age and benefit from seeing mission teams sent out, especially to Montreal, where I would be baptized nine years later.

The catalyst for me to seek God was when my boyfriend broke up with me in 1996. Our relationship was far from perfect, as there had been surprises. One surprise was that he had a son. He hid it from me as he did not want that to be the deciding factor of our relationship, even though I had made it clear that it would be. When I came back to Canada to deal with some issues with my scholarship, he ended things. He had decided to try and make it work with the mother of his child.

I was devastated. My stepmother took me out to a movie and let me sleep in her room, while my dad was out of town working. I would cry at night and she would comfort me. Her care for me and pointing me toward God helped my heart. One day, my dad was back in town, sat with me, and showed me the Scripture that I will never forget. To this day, it remains a pivotal Scripture in my life:

> *What causes fights and quarrels among you? Don't they come from your desires that battle within you? You desire but do not have, so you kill. You covet but you cannot get what*

you want, so you quarrel and fight. You do not have because you do not ask God. When you ask, you do not receive, because you ask with wrong motives, that you may spend what you get on your pleasures.

You adulterous people, don't you know that friendship with the world means enmity against God? Therefore, anyone who chooses to be a friend of the world becomes an enemy of God. Or do you think Scripture says without reason that He jealously longs for the spirit He has caused to dwell in us? But He gives us more grace. That is why Scripture says:

"God opposes the proud but shows favor to the humble."

Submit yourselves, then, to God. Resist the Devil, and he will flee from you. Come near to God and He will come near to you. Wash your hands, you sinners, and purify your hearts, you double-minded. Grieve, mourn and wail. Change your laughter to mourning and your joy to gloom. Humble yourselves before the Lord, and He will lift you up. (James 4:1-10)

That was the moment the Bible "clicked" in my head and heart. I had wanted the relationship with my boyfriend so badly that I had been praying empty prayers to God for it to work out long term to marriage. It was not until my father began to read that Scripture that I was amazed at how relevant the Bible was and how much it exposed my heart's inner motives.

I took great pains in painting a particular picture of myself that would please my parents, even though I lived in secret sin. I could not believe that the Bible was so adept at exposing the raw truth of my ungodly life. I wanted the relationship not because I cared about what was best for my boyfriend, not because I cared about using it to honor God, but simply because *"I"* wanted it.

That was the very first time I can remember the Bible discipling the motives of my heart. It changed my life. I was in self-preservation mode: I wanted to preserve my happiness at the expense of another. It had not occurred to me that his son might desire to have a chance to have his mother and father make it work. I had my own selfish agenda.

It was at that moment I decided to study the Bible. I remember going to the house of the Montreal Women's Ministry Leader to do *The Cross Study*. As I walked from one side of the street to the other, I remember praying in my head, "Please, God, don't let me get hit by a car right now because if I die, I am going to hell." I understood the seriousness of my position before God, and I wanted to remedy it as soon as possible!

Thankfully, God listened to my prayer and I was baptized on January 29, 1997. I was so grateful for my sins being washed away! I felt the endearing closeness of God and the inexpressible joy of my salvation. Sadly, while I was grateful for obeying the Scriptures and receiving the forgiveness of my sins, I had deceived myself into thinking that I could manipulate God.

The Author graduated from Lester B. Pearson Catholic High School in 1996, less than one year before becoming a disciple.

After finishing *The Cross Study* and confessing my sin, I secretly prayed to God to convert my ex-boyfriend. He had tried to "make it work" with the mother of his child, but that plan failed. He then decided to move to Los Angeles. I believed that somehow if I was baptized, God would answer my prayer if I accompanied it with fasting. So, I fasted and prayed as a young disciple to help my "ex" become a Christian. Satan's timing, as usual, was flawless.

Like Lot's wife, I had tried to "go back" for what to me was an Earthly possession. I wanted to keep this part of my life, thinly veiled by me convincing myself that it was for the glory of God when it was only for me. And so, I manipulated situations around me on a quest to get what I wanted.

My "Lot's wife moment" arose when my dad and his family moved to Indonesia for work. My eldest sister and I were going to visit for a month. After seeing our flight itinerary, I knew now was my chance or never. My "ex" lived in Los Angeles when I searched for ways to stop over in LA. I told myself that my cousin lived there, and now that I was a disciple, she could come to church with me. Not only that, I could also get my ex to go to church with us and study the Bible… and get baptized.

Feeling "spiritual," I decided that it was God's will and so convinced my dad to get our return flights from Indonesia to stop over in Los Angeles before heading back to Canada. It worked! My sister had to head back, but I managed to stay for a couple of weeks in Los Angeles without her.

We contacted our family and set up a time to spend together. I also contacted my ex-boyfriend and set up a time to meet. When he voiced a mutual desire to meet, I was so happy. I remember thinking, yes, this must be what God wants because He would not allow this meeting to take place otherwise. Visions of him going to church with me and being impacted by seeing the Kingdom of God played in my head. Afternoons of him studying the Bible, crying over the Scriptures, and finally standing over the waters of baptism shouting, "Jesus is Lord," were all of which I could think.

This would happen only because of my faith and perseverance. We would date purely, and he would propose, and of course, I would say, "Yes!" We would be married and serve as an example to so many of the power of God. It was all for God, I would remind myself.

I was only 19. It was my second relationship in my young life and, up until that moment, my first real love. He was six years older, and to me, he was larger than life. I was so young. I thought I knew what real love was, and though I was not malicious in my endeavor, I thought I could manipulate God to achieve "my dream."

My ex did come to church. When church was over - in the car - I asked him what he had thought of it. He was noncommittal. I pressed the subject, and he ended up confessing that he was not interested. I asked him if he would study the Bible. Again, the response was vague. My heart sank. I was in disbelief. I got angry with him. We argued. I could not believe it. After all my prayers, all my fasting, all my planning and hard work to get him to see the Kingdom of God, he did not want to study the Bible.

My motives revealed themselves, and I became desperate. My desperation led me to give in to sin. Thankfully, before anything irreversible took place, I came to my senses. The entire truth was revealed at that moment, as he confessed to being in a relationship with another woman. So, there I was, a young disciple of only four months, devastated once again.

Not only had my entire plan utterly failed, but it also led me to the sin of impurity with my ex... sadly as a Christian.

I remember being at my cousin's apartment (she was attending UCLA at the time) and crying over Ephesians 1:3-14. To have my heart broken twice by the same person I felt was too much for me to bear. Not only that, but this second time had caused me to stumble in my walk with God in a significant way.

As the tears flowed down my cheeks, my eyes kept going over this passage in Ephesians:

> *For He chose us in Him before the creation of the world to be holy and blameless in His sight. In love He predestined us for adoption to sonship through Jesus Christ, in accordance with His pleasure and will - to the praise of His glorious grace, which He has freely given us in the One He loves. In Him we have redemption through His blood, the forgiveness of sins, in accordance with the riches of God's grace that He lavished on us. With all wisdom and understanding.* (Ephesians 1:4-8)

As a guilty soul, I was so grateful for God's grace to completely forgive me of my longing for the world through deceitful planning and gross impurity. This amazing passage went on:

> *In Him we were also chosen, having been predestined according to the plan of Him who*

> *works out everything in conformity with the purpose of His will, in order that we, who were the first to put our hope in Christ, might be for the praise of His glory. And you also were included in Christ when you heard the message of truth, the gospel of your salvation. When you believed, you were marked in Him with a seal, the promised Holy Spirit, who is a deposit guaranteeing our inheritance until the redemption of those who are God's possession - to the praise of His glory.* (Ephesians 1:11-14)

The idea that I was a significant part of God's plan to become a disciple of Jesus, receiving the forgiveness of my sins and the Holy Spirit guaranteeing my inheritance, broke my heart. Why would God be so gracious and generous when I had treated Him like a genie from whom I could exact wishes? After everything, I finally sought comfort and solace in God as my great reward. (Genesis 15:1)

In flying back to Montreal, I cried all the way home on the plane. Upon landing, I immediately confessed in tears what had happened to my sister and my discipler right away. In gentleness and love, they listened and were able to help me see what happened in my heart. I remember sharing and feeling relief and a sense of closure.

To try and hold on to my old life, I had come dangerously close to losing my salvation. My eyes were opened. In my longing for the world, I had tried to force something that, upon reflection, was not an honest or pure relationship. Of course, God did not bless it! It contradicted my prayer that

I made the night of my baptism: "God do whatever you need to do to keep me faithful for the rest of my life."

After seven years as a disciple, the Author graduated from Concordia University in 2003. Celebrating this milestone are the Author's stepmother Brigitte and her elder sister Tamara, the women who baptized her!

While I thought I had experienced my first real love, it was nothing compared to meeting and falling in love with my future husband. I am so grateful for my husband, Tim. God answered my prayer through him. He is faithful and fights to help me stay close to God, guides and teaches me, and strives to be an example that I can follow. There is a song that I used to love that now perfectly describes my husband, sung by Ben Harper entitled, *Gold To Me,*

> *I've been fooled before*
> *But now I know*
> *I've made the mistake in the past*
> *But now I know the difference*
> *From gold and brass.*

As a 19-year old young woman, I was still chasing brass, longing for the past, not knowing that God wanted me to have pure gold in a godly man like my husband. To my shame, like Lot's wife, I looked back.

The very first time that I met Tim was after church at lunch. My campus household hosted this particular lunch, and some disciples came over. One of my good friends brought his guest with him, a tall red-headed "campus guy." I remember being friendly but appropriately keeping my distance. Interestingly, the young man struck up a conversation with me. And so, we talked, and he told me about so many different ideas he had. I nodded and smiled but tried to keep from getting "too into" the conversation, as I did not want to give him the wrong idea.

He came out to more and more events and studied the Bible. Then the day came for him to be baptized. I remember going to the baptism and seeing him there, looking so nervous and a little scared. Before Tim's baptism, he shared with all in attendance that he had been concerned that he would not make it to his baptism. Tim expressed that he could not believe he could have salvation after the life he had led. After his baptism, we all went up to the brother's apartment and celebrated. I remember Tim was so encouraged!

We were going to the same college, so we would often get together in the coffee shop to study as a campus ministry. We grew to know one another better and better, and eventually became very good friends. We talked about God, about school, family, our old lives and our dreams.

I remember the day that I realized that I liked him. I was working in the office of the registrar at my university sorting letters in the file room and it hit me: I liked Tim Kernan. I was shocked. He was so different from other interests that I had in the past, but there was something about his devotion to God that inspired me.

The Author on a date with her boyfriend and future husband, Tim.

One Sunday after church, Tim said something that made my heart sink. He wanted to be an evangelist. My heart sank because I did not think that ministry was my path. I had already dated someone in the church who had broken up with me because he thought I was not "destined for the ministry." So, I figured that I might as well get rid of my feelings to avoid a similar heartbreak.

As time went on, I found that I could not move on. What's more, I sensed that the feeling was mutual. I was terrified to give my heart. I had made so many worldly choices in the past that I did not trust myself. I did not want to have wrong motives. I prayed for clarity and for God to make it obvious, without any interference from me.

One day, my discipler asked me how I would feel about potentially building with Tim. I was floored. I immediately said, "Yes!" It makes me laugh at how shocked I was and how right it felt. That following Sunday afternoon, all of the teens were at Tim's and the guys' household, and I went along with some other sisters from church. He was not saying anything, but I knew that he knew. And so, I decided to ask if he had talked with his discipler lately.

That conversation confirmed for me that Tim was the one for whom I was waiting. He told me he was "crazy about me" and that we would date but that we needed to do things right. That moment began an adventure that I would never have seen coming. The course of my life changed that day… for eternity.

Since being married to Tim on November 1, 2003, God has called us to leave many homes and give up many things in the past 17 years. With the Spirit guiding us, Tim and I have moved from Montreal to Toronto to Los Angeles to London back to Los Angeles to Paris to Syracuse again back to Los Angeles to Chennai to Paris again to Los Angeles, then back to Toronto and finally returning to Los Angeles.

Rather than "settling for Zoar," Tim and I moved "to the mountains" thirteen times in 17 years! I would always get my heart surrendered to move, but it was not always comfortable. Some of our moves were easy, but others were slightly nerve-racking. That being said, I can always count on Tim to "go to the mountains" without hesitation!

The Author on her glorious wedding day!

While I have a deep conviction that God and not man determines my steps, there have been times that I have been tempted to plead with God for a more comfortable cross. There have been a few days when I have even been tempted to look back, longing for my old life.

Reminiscing can become an idol in our hearts. We can live so much in the past that it can destroy our future. We become paralyzed and unable to move forward. When God has told us to go to cities of all shapes and kinds, beautiful and not so beautiful, it can be tempting to revert to worldly thinking. We can desire convenience and comfort like Lot's wife, who was looking back.

Another less talked about desire we can look back to is romantic fantasies of past relationships and even imaginary relationships. Emotional affairs are a widespread struggle among women. Disturbingly, Christian women can be vulnerable to this as well. An article on *Fatherly.com* has this to say:

> Most people have committed emotional infidelity at some point - an affair of the heart, without physically cheating on a significant other - and women may cheat more than men. Research involving 90,000 men and women found that 78.6 percent of men and 91.6 percent of women admitted to having an emotional affair.
>
> One reason women may be more likely to have emotional affairs is similar to the reason men are more likely to cheat physically. Men tend to have more physical needs, whereas women have more emotional ones. "Emotional affairs are often the result of people acting out in ways that allow them to endure and tolerate the painful feelings of being isolated in long-term love."[25]

How heart-breaking. To endure, so many women resort to engaging in an affair in their mind. This imaginary partner meets all of their emotional needs and becomes a place of comfort and refuge. Often, becoming a Christian and marrying a godly man eliminates this emotional crutch until

---

[25]https://www.fatherly.com/health-science/emotional-affair/

one finds themselves at a challenging time in their relationship with their spouse. Inevitably, the desire to "turn back" to the emotional affair, be it an imaginary partner or a co-worker, or friend, becomes irresistible. This emotional affair can eventually steal from their real relationship, rendering it a loveless partnership that, if not dealt with, can lead to the death of the actual relationship.

What is the Biblical solution to this dilemma with which all too many women wrestle? When we say the words, *"Jesus is Lord,"* we are entering into a master-servant relationship with Him. We crucify our independent spirits and look for ways to live for Christ and not for ourselves. Jesus calls us to leave the elements of our past that we used to hold on to that were not beneficial. Whatever we formerly held on to in place of God was destined for destruction the moment we were baptized. The search for personal comfort over others' spiritual needs can trap us and keep us from living life to the full.

In an article posted by the newspaper *Picayune Item* entitled, *Don't Run Back Into A Burning House,* the staff reporter writes the following:

> Unfortunately, there are a few would-be survivors every year who perish because they ran back into a burning home to retrieve something.
>
> On February 7th, Sandy McCullar, a 57-year-old woman from Bruce, Mississippi died after running back into her house to save her cats.

While she managed to rescue her pets, she experienced several third-degree burns and had to be rushed by helicopter to a hospital, according to coverage by Associated Press. Sadly, she passed away later that afternoon.

The National Fire Protection Association website states that once away from a burning building, it is imperative to stay outside.

"Under no circumstances should you ever go back into a burning building," an article on the site states… "Tell a firefighter instead of attempting a rescue yourself." The same is true for material possessions.[26]

In this article, there is a striking parallel in the way we look at our relationship with God. When we become disciples, we become part of God's church, the bride of Christ! As the bride, when things get challenging, we must avoid the temptation to become embroiled in an emotional affair with the world and the things of the world. The solutions to overcoming longing for the world are honesty, obedience to God's Word, concentrating on being grateful, and having a Heavenly focus.

> *Brothers and sisters, I do not consider myself yet to have taken hold of it. But one thing I do: Forgetting what is behind and straining toward*

---

[26] http://www.picayuneitem.com/2018/02/dont-run-back-into-a-burning-house/

> *what is ahead, I press on toward the goal to win the prize for which God has called me Heavenward in Christ Jesus.* (Philippians 3:12-14)

It is impossible to successfully move forward in life if we are continually dwelling on our past accomplishments, longings, failures or circumstances. We must always strive to move forward, or even as one author put it, "fail forward." As Jesus said, *"No one who puts a hand to the plow and looks back is fit for service in the Kingdom of God."* (Luke 9:62) Looking back means destruction.

Loving the world compared to loving God is illustrated emphatically in the following passage:

> *If they have escaped the corruption of the world by knowing our Lord and Savior Jesus Christ and are again entangled in it and are overcome, they are worse off at the end than they were at the beginning. It would have been better for them not to have known the way of righteousness, than to have known it and then to turn their backs on the sacred command that was passed on to them. Of them the proverbs are true: "A dog returns to its vomit," and, "A sow that is washed returns to her wallowing in the mud."* (2 Peter 2: 20-22)

When we are tempted to look back like Lot's wife, we must strongly resist the urge, knowing where it will lead us spiritually.

> *Do not love the world or the things in the world. If anyone loves the world, the love of the Father is not in Him. For all that is in the world - the desires of the flesh and the desires of the eyes and pride in possessions - is not from the Father but is from the world. And the world is passing away along with its desires, but whoever does the will of God abides forever.* (1 John 2:15-17 ESV)

There are so many Scriptures on this topic because it is so close to God's heart. God demands that we do not lust for the world and become spiritual pillars of salt.

> *"You adulterous people! Do you not know that friendship with the world is enmity with God? Therefore whoever wishes to be a friend of the world makes himself an enemy of God."* (James 4:4)

When we begin an emotional affair with the world, it eventually will lead to our love for God growing cold. We ultimately become His enemy. This is how blind we can become. It is easy to become mesmerized by the world and begin walking down the wrong path.

Lot's wife had become conformed to the world. God was calling her to lose her life to save it. Interestingly, the act of starting over and not allowing ourselves to be owned by our belongings keeps us in a place where the trap of greed and materialism unclouds us. Money and belongings have their place and are not bad in and of themselves, but as Christians, they must never take God's place.

> *"For the love of money is a root of all kinds of evils. It is through this craving that some have wandered away from the faith and pierced themselves with many pangs."* (1 Timothy 6:10 ESV)

An emotional affair with money is one of the most enticing temptations that can pull people away from God.

> *"No one can serve two masters, for either he will hate the one and love the other, or he will be devoted to the one and despise the other. You cannot serve God and money."* (Matthew 6:24 ESV)

God wants to have a vibrant, dynamic and pure relationship with us. He is jealous for us and notices when we go astray. *"For I feel a divine jealousy for you, since I betrothed you to one husband, to present you as a pure virgin to Christ."* (2 Corinthians 11:2 ESV)

The Paper Tiger of Longing for the World is overcome with truth. The illusion of the world is powerful, but we must use Scripture to remind us what the world truly is. It takes courage to examine where we stand, and it takes "guts" to put the world in its appropriate place in our lives. While we must live in the world, we must not love it more than God.

> *Everyone who believes that Jesus is the Christ is born of God, and everyone who loves the father loves His child as well. This is how we know that we love the children of God: by*

> *loving God and carrying out His commands. In fact, this is love for God: to keep His commands. And His commands are not burdensome, for everyone born of God overcomes the world. This is the victory that has overcome the world, even our faith. Who is it that overcomes the world? Only the one who believes that Jesus is the Son of God.* (1 John 5:1-5)

When I reflect on Lot's wife, I feel for her because she and I are the same. I have been tempted to look back. I have, at times, fallen into the trap of longing for aspects of my old life. I have been tempted to forsake my first love. As Lot's wife became a pillar of salt for her choices, I must be aware that I am responsible for the choices that I make and the consequences.

I am thankful to God that through Christ there is repentance and second chances, third chances, fourth chances... We can overcome and be victorious. We can set an example of faith and fortitude for the women who will look to us for an example of godly women - not seduced by the pull of the world - but strengthened and motivated by the blood of Christ.

"After being diagnosed with bone cancer, I was not afraid to die because I believe in Heaven. Now I realize that every day is a gift from God."

Dr. Elena Garcia McKean

Paper Tiger Five
The Bleeding Woman's Suffering

Jesus Healing the Bleeding Woman
Paolo Veronese (1565-70)

And a woman was there who had been subject to bleeding for twelve years, but no one could heal her. She came up behind Him and touched the edge of His cloak, and immediately her bleeding stopped.

"Who touched me?" Jesus asked.

When they all denied it, Peter said, "Master, the people are crowding and pressing against you."

But Jesus said, "Someone touched me; I know that power has gone out from me."

> *Then the woman, seeing that she could not go unnoticed, came trembling and fell at His feet. In the presence of all the people, she told why she had touched Him and how she had been instantly healed. Then He said to her, "Daughter, your faith has healed you. Go in peace."* (Luke 8:43-48)

In all three Synoptic Gospels, the Bleeding Woman was recorded as suffering for 12 long years. For over a decade, she visited physicians who were unable to help her. In this empty pursuit, the Bleeding Woman *"had spent all she had."* (Mark 5:26)

According to Leviticus 15, a woman's monthly period made her unclean until seven days afterward. Anyone who touched her would be regarded as unclean as well until the end of the day. (Leviticus 15:19, 25, 27) As a result, this condition required the Bleeding Woman to be separated from the people. Twelve years later, the isolation, save the company of doctors, would have been terrible.

The hem of Jesus' robe was Biblically significant.

> *The Lord said to Moses, "Speak to the Israelites and say to them: 'Throughout the generations to come you are to make tassels on the corners of your garments, with a blue cord on each tassel. You will have these tassels to look at and so you will remember all the commands of the Lord, that you may obey them and not prostitute yourselves by chasing*

> *after the lusts of your own hearts and eyes.'"*
> (Numbers 15:37-39)

The tassels were meant to remind all Jewish men that those who wore them were set apart and were to obey God's Law. However, we do not know if Jesus did have tassels or not. By noting that it was the hem of Jesus' cloak, which the woman touches, this indeed was an act of humility before one she considered much more significant than herself.

The Bleeding Woman
Catacombs of Marcellinus and Peter (400 AD)

Robes and tassels were very consequential in the time of Jesus. Of the Pharisees' robes Jesus said, *"They do all their deeds to be seen by others. For they make their phylacteries broad and their fringes long..."* (Matthew 23:5) For Jesus, robes, fringes and accouterments were not as important as the actual spiritual heart.

It is fascinating to note that the crowd jostling around Jesus had an intense level of contact with Him. Yet because their touch was involuntary and without purpose, nothing miraculous happened. They literally did not "grasp" the power before them.

The Bleeding Woman, on the other hand, was very purposeful. Jesus immediately recognized her touch of hope and faith as He felt the power go out from Him. (Luke 8:46) Her desperation to be healed led to an act of courage that changed the course of her life. She reached out to Jesus for physical healing just as we do for spiritual healing today.

Jesus lived in a world of extremes - enormous wealth and crippling poverty, which accentuated every day's misery. Likewise, those of us in the first world know very well it too is full of suffering. Nevertheless, it is carefully masked, medicated and muted. In contrast, suffering is in full view in the developing third world and was a constant in Jesus' travels.

I had no idea of the anguish people felt until I had the opportunity to visit Chennai, India. Of all the places Tim and I served as missionaries, this was the one place that brought the Scriptures' setting most to life. We lived there for three months with our two young children.

It was beautiful to be serving the Lord in India among the extraordinary disciples. It was incredible to be teaching and preaching and encouraging the wonderful Chennai Church!

The Author's sons with the precious children of the Chennai Church!

During that time, I was always concerned with the welfare of my children. Toddlers, as you know, get into everything everywhere. I was always on the lookout for anything my youngest son David could put into his mouth or touch. Then one night, I felt the beginning of a fever.

I thought to myself, "Oops, it looks like I might have caught a cold from someone or something." I thought nothing of it and instead just went to bed in the hope that sleep would help. The following day, the feeling still lingered. I felt worse as the day went on, although not yet intolerable.

By day three, I was feverish. My lower back and kidneys were aching, and my eyes hurt whenever I tried to look up. For a moment, I thought, "Could it be meningitis?" We went to the clinic, and the doctor gave me some paracetamol (similar to Tylenol) and an injection that began to reduce the fever within 20 minutes. I thought to myself, "Thank goodness! I can go home and take care of my children!" Unfortunately for me, it would take much more than paracetamol to cure what was quickly spreading in my blood.

I took the pills from the doctor regularly and I slept for hours on end. Instead of getting better, I returned to the state I was in before I saw the doctor. No amount of sleep was enough. The paracetamol would break the fever, but it did not last. The fatigue was constant. I could not eat. Then came the sweating. Every morning, my pillow would be drenched in sweat.

I was worried that what I had was contagious, so I removed myself from the rest of the family. I moved to the living room couch. An added benefit was that the couch was softer than the bed. However, I spent the entire night tossing and turning, sweating and listless. My fever was so high that I became delirious. I was afraid.

I started to wonder if I was dying. I did not want my family to wake the next morning and find that I had died. All I could do was to pray, as I went in and out of consciousness.

One morning, I woke up extremely weak. I could barely hold up my head. It had been five days of not being able to ingest anything. At the same time, Tim Junior also began exhibiting similar symptoms. There is nothing worse for a mother than seeing her child ill and not having the strength to take care of him. Thank goodness for Tim, who did an outstanding job of taking care of the boys while still striving to help the Chennai Church.

That night "Auntie Grandma June" - a wonderful mature woman from the Chennai Church - stayed home with the children while Tim took me to the emergency room of a nearby hospital. I was nervous as they took my blood for testing. I was even more unnerved by the presence of mosquitoes everywhere. The nurse that first attempted to administer the IV left me screaming as she tried multiple times to jab the needle into my vein. When she was unsuccessful, she reasoned that more force would do the trick. It did not.

They left me alone for a little while, and I could not help it; I put my hands over my face, and I cried. The entire environment overwhelmed me. It was late. I was tired, and my son was at home with a fever.

I prayed to God without words. Thank God for Johnny and Leno Agnal, who came with us to the hospital. Leno is a nurse and was able to make sure that things were done correctly going forward. Finally, another more experienced worker came and expertly put the IV into my other hand while Tim comforted me and kept me calm. They hydrated me and gave me antibiotics.

After a few hours, the doctor came to see me. He told us that I had tested positive for Dengue Fever. Tim and I were unsure of how to respond. We had never heard of Dengue

Fever. When Johnny and Leno listened to the medical report, their reaction concerned us, and so we looked online for information on the disease. What we discovered shocked us: "The Dengue virus is the leading cause of illness and death in the tropics and subtropics."[27]

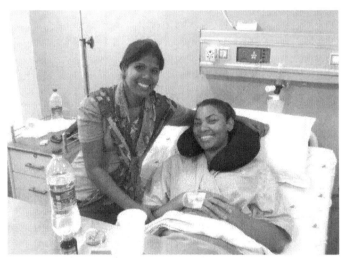

In 2013, Maria - a sister in the Chennai Church - helped to nurse the Author to health, as she was recovering from Dengue Fever.

Dengue can be a fatal sickness transmitted most commonly by mosquitos. It is an illness that causes the blood vessels to leak blood.[28] I would never have imagined that a mosquito bite could leave Tim a widower, and my children without a mother.

---

[27]https://www.cdc.gov/dengue/index.html
[28]https://www.cdc.gov/dengue/index.html

I remember looking around at the dozens of people in beds with all manner of illnesses. I could sense their suffering and hopelessness. I too felt afraid, as I was far from home, and my body was failing to respond to the initial treatments.

Thank God for the sisters in the Chennai Church. They never left my side, all the while taking turns being with me and feeding me. They even stayed overnight. This fellowship helped me to fight to keep positive.

The Author with Debs Rajan and the amazing sisters in the Chennai Church!

That first night in the hospital room, however, my resolve was shattered. Tim called me at 2:30 AM and said that he was taking Junior to the emergency room. I just cried. What could I do? I knew they would put an IV into his hand and that he would be so scared, and I could not be there with him. How long would Junior be hospitalized? And David? What would happen to 19-month-old David?

From that moment on, I withdrew into myself. The sisters were with me, but I felt so tempted to give into the feeling of hopelessness. The immensity of the cultural chasm - and my inability to be with my husband and children - accentuated this disorienting feeling all the more. I was eye to eye with the Paper Tiger of Suffering. All I could do was read and listen to my Bible non-stop to keep from falling apart. I must have come across as very anti-social, but I was fighting to cope with the seemingly overwhelming circumstances.

Thankfully, after being rehydrated, Tim reported that Junior began to improve. Raja and Debs Rajan - the hospitable Chennai Church Leaders - took David into their home all that week and took excellent care of him for us. It always brings tears to my eyes when I think of what the Rajans did for us by caring for David. I will be forever grateful to them and their children Ashwin, Shefali and Isheeta, who welcomed David into their family.

The doctors did blood tests to determine whether or not I would need a blood transfusion. Typically, an average white platelet count is between 150,000 and 450,000, but mine dropped to 65,000. My platelet level, while low, had not fallen to the point of needing a blood transfusion. I prayed that my body would fight. Thankfully, the treatment worked, and my body slowly began to improve.

After being in the hospital for almost a week, I was well enough to go home. It was so good to be out and to walk in the fresh air! I had not seen my children in five days. It took about another week to return to full strength, but praise God, He sent His angels to be by my side and allowed me to recover fully.

David adored "Debs Auntie."

Being so sick helped to sober me and deepened my convictions. As a Westerner, I learned that what I experienced staying in the hospital was simply life in the third world. This experience has impacted me to this day. It put my first world problems into a sharp and very different perspective. Living in India convicted me of what the definition of a "problem" really was. The incredible Indian disciples were able to rejoice and find joy even in difficulties as they practiced Scriptures such as:

> *I am not saying this because I am in need, for I have learned to be content whatever the circumstances. I know what it is to be in need, and I know what it is to have plenty. I have learned the secret of being content in any and every situation, whether well fed or hungry, whether living in plenty or in want. I can do all this through Him who gives me strength.*
> (Philippians 4:11-13)

Paul shared a fundamental principle with the Philippians that everyone needs to grasp in a world of suffering and problems. We must all eventually face issues that do not just "go away." ***"The secret to being content in every situation"*** is very simple: Go to Jesus who gives us strength.

What was God teaching me through my medical trials? He taught me to depend on Him. Sometimes one needs to have a near-death experience to really depend on the Lord. This Scripture came alive for me:

> *And He humbled you and let you hunger and fed you with manna, which you did not know, nor did your fathers know, that He might make you know that man does not live by bread alone, but man lives by every word that comes from the mouth of the Lord.* (Deuteronomy 8:3 ESV)

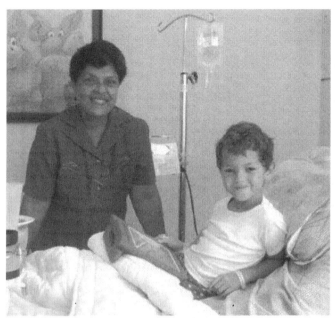

The Author's son Tim Junior was visited many
times by "Auntie Grandma June"
in the children's ward.

When every "good thing" is gone, the only "good things" left are God and His Word. Indeed, we do not need bread as much as we need God's Word in times of hardship.

"Many are the afflictions of the righteous, but the Lord delivers him out of them all." (Psalm 34:19 ESV) God allows us to go through so much, but we can always trust Him! *"Before I was afflicted I went astray, but now I keep your Word... It is good for me that I was afflicted, that I might learn your statutes."* (Psalm 119:67, 71 ESV) Suffering is sometimes the only way we learn to obey God and His marvelous commands.

Jesus was a man of suffering. *"He was despised and rejected by men; a man of sorrows, and acquainted with grief; and as one from whom men hide their faces He was despised, and we esteemed Him not."* (Isaiah 53:3 ESV) Therefore why should we think that we will not suffer as well? *"For to this you have been called, because Christ also suffered for you, leaving you an example, so that you might follow in His steps."* (1 Peter 2:21 ESV)

Yet when we suffer "as" Jesus did, we must suffer "like" Jesus did.

> *And going a little farther, He fell on the ground and prayed that, if it were possible, the hour might pass from Him. And He said, "Abba, Father, all things are possible for you. Remove this cup from me. Yet not what I will, but what you will."* (Mark 14:35-36 ESV)

When Jesus suffered, He did it with reverence and respect for God, not self-pity, blame-shifting or hopelessness. Jesus warns us that we will have similar problems to Him. *"I have said these things to you, that in me you may have peace. In the world you will have tribulation. But take heart; I have overcome the world."* (John 16:33 ESV)

Suffering gives us encouraging qualities such as endurance, character and hope. A deep sense of trust and expectation that something good will happen is so important to cultivate to have sincere hope.

> *More than that, we rejoice in our sufferings, knowing that suffering produces endurance,*

and endurance produces character, and character produces hope, and hope does not put us to shame, because God's love has been poured into our hearts through the Holy Spirit who has been given to us. (Romans 5:3-5 ESV)

Fighting against the darkness and the pain in this world becomes worth it when we think about God's amazing blessings in store for us. *"For I consider that the sufferings of this present time are not worth comparing with the glory that is to be revealed to us."* (Romans 8:18 ESV) This is the attitude we must continue to refine. *"For this light momentary affliction is preparing for us an eternal weight of glory beyond all comparison..."* (2 Corinthians 4:17 ESV)

Junior celebrated his fourth birthday in Chennai!

Sometimes when we go through trouble, it is because we are in sin and separated from God. However, this is not always the case. *"Who shall separate us from the love of Christ?*

Shall tribulation, or distress, or persecution, or famine, or nakedness, or danger, or sword?" (Romans 8:35 ESV) Often when we go through hardship in this broken world, God is not against us but for us. In our suffering, which brings maturity, He is there to comfort us.

> *Blessed be the God and Father of our Lord Jesus Christ, the Father of mercies and God of all comfort, who comforts us in all our affliction, so that we may be able to comfort those who are in any affliction, with the comfort with which we ourselves are comforted by God.* (2 Corinthians 1:3-4 ESV)

God gives His unique comfort amid difficulties. *"For we do not have a high priest who is unable to sympathize with our weaknesses, but one who in every respect has been tempted as we are, yet without sin."* (Hebrews 4:15 ESV) Since Jesus suffered as we did, we can be assured that God is full of compassion and sympathy as we go through suffering.

This mix of suffering, rejoicing and comfort gives us strength! Paul wrote, *"We are afflicted in every way, but not crushed; perplexed, but not driven to despair; persecuted, but not forsaken; struck down, but not destroyed; always carrying in the body the death of Jesus, so that the life of Jesus may also be manifested in our bodies."* (2 Corinthians 4:8-10 ESV)

Sometimes God allows suffering to keep us humble as He did with Paul, one of the strongest of Christians. Paul shares about this in 2 Corinthians 12:7, *"So to keep me from becoming conceited because of the surpassing greatness of the revelations, a thorn was given me in the flesh, a messenger of Satan to harass me, to keep me from becoming conceited."*

God is watching us and helping us, so that we do not become sinful and go to the place of eternal suffering. (Matthew 25:46) That is not the kind of suffering we would wish on anyone.

One of the most important coping mechanisms is friendship. *"Bear one another's burdens, and so fulfill the law of Christ."* (Galatians 6:2 ESV) Tim says, "It is not good for a man to be alone - but it is also not good for a woman to be alone with a man. You need other female friends." Sisterhood is so important.

That special "sisterhood fellowship" comes from being open with one another in our difficulties and rejoicing in our victories. As the Scripture says, *"But if we walk in the light, as He is in the light, we have fellowship with one another, and the blood of Jesus, His Son, purifies us from all sin."* (1 John 1:7) Every so often, I take the time to make a detailed sin list, as well as a list of things for which I am grateful. By sharing this with select other sisters and sharing their lists with each other and me, this openness draws us all closer together.

When we first try to be open about where we are, what can creep into our hearts is to "clean up" the truth a bit to make it less alarming. To get "the best of both worlds" in forgiveness from God and gaining fellowship, we end up gaining neither. Most people can tell when we are holding back. Even if they cannot put their finger on precisely what the problem is, we can feel when there is a lack of realness.

The Kernan family visited the Taj Mahal in Agra, India - one of the Seven Wonders of the World.

It takes courage to confess. The reward of real transparency and telling the whole truth is that there is no longer anything to hide or fear. There is freedom and peace because there is not the lingering anxiety of having to "cover our tracks." Decide to be utterly truthful before God and with your closest disciple friends.

We cannot be "caught off guard" by the Paper Tiger of Suffering. The Bible says, *"Beloved, do not be surprised at the fiery trial when it comes upon you to test you, as though something strange were happening to you. But rejoice insofar as you share Christ's sufferings, that you may also rejoice and be glad when his glory is revealed. If you are insulted for the name of Christ, you are blessed, because the Spirit of glory and of God rests upon you. But let none of you suffer as a murderer or a thief or an evildoer or as a meddler. Yet if anyone suffers as a Christian, let him not be ashamed, but let him glorify God in that name."* (1 Peter 4:12-19 ESV)

In the end, the Bleeding Woman found healing because of her faith. Her isolation due to her being unclean made her desperate for a cure. Despite the Bleeding Woman's fear of coming forward, she fell at Jesus's feet and shared the whole truth with Him. As Christian women, we have also been healed by Jesus. In turn, we must become women who will provide others a safe place, so they too can "fall at Jesus's feet" and be healed by the grace of God.

I am grateful for my terrible times. The joy Jesus gave me during my suffering produced perseverance, which strengthened my character. *"In this you rejoice, though now for a little while, if necessary, you have been grieved by various trials, so that the tested genuineness of your faith - more precious than gold that perishes though it is tested by fire - may be found to result in praise and glory and honor at the revelation of Jesus Christ."* (1 Peter 1:6-7 ESV)

I am so grateful that God has allowed me to be a missionary. The experiences that I have had taught me so much about relying on the infinite power of God. I pray I waste no experience - past or future. I pray that God uses all of my sufferings to continue to convict my heart and keep me grateful. As a disciple of Jesus, I know trials and challenges will come, and along with them, the Paper Tiger of Suffering. After all, each bout of suffering is preparing us for the next bout... which in time prepares us to enter Heaven.

"He will wipe away every tear from their eyes, and death shall be no more, neither shall there be mourning, nor crying, nor pain anymore, for the former things have passed away." (Revelation 21:4 ESV)

"I get up and pace the room as if I can leave my guilt behind me. But it tracks me as I walk, an ugly shadow made by myself."

Rosamund Lupton

Paper Tiger Six
The Adulterous Woman's Guilty Feelings

Christ and the Woman Taken in Adultery
Nicolas Poussin (1653)

> At dawn He appeared again in the temple courts, where all the people gathered around Him, and He sat down to teach them. The teachers of the Law and the Pharisees brought in a woman caught in adultery. They made her stand before the group and said to Jesus, "Teacher, this woman was caught in the act of adultery. In the Law, Moses commanded us to stone such women. Now what do you say?" They were using this question as a trap, in order to have a basis for accusing Him. (John 8:1-6a)

In this account, the Adulterous Woman was dragged out into the public arena to be condemned. The Pharisees asked Jesus if the woman should be stoned, in an attempt to trap Him in His words. It was a very intense moment.

> *But Jesus bent down and started to write on the ground with His finger. When they kept on questioning Him, He straightened up and said to them, "Let anyone of you who is without sin be the first to throw a stone at her." Again He stooped down and wrote on the ground.* (John 8:6b-8)

Surprisingly, Jesus responded to the challenge of the Pharisees by writing on the ground. One cannot help but wonder what He was writing. What the Pharisees did not realize about Jesus is that in trying to trap Him, they would only be trapping themselves.

> *At this, those who heard began to go away one at a time, the older ones first, until only Jesus was left, with the woman still standing there. Jesus straightened up and asked her, "Woman, where are they? Has no one condemned you?"*
>
> *"No one, sir," she said.*
>
> *"Then neither do I condemn you," Jesus declared. "Go now and leave your life of sin."* (John 8:9-11)

For the Adulterous Woman, her moment of condemnation becomes her moment of freedom. The forgiveness of Jesus washed away her guilt as He challenged the religious leaders on theirs. This was a profound scene. Without Jesus, this woman would have died a terrible death. In my mind, I think that when Jesus stooped down, He might have written something to this effect, *"If a man is found sleeping with another man's wife, both the man who slept with her and the woman must die."* (Deuteronomy 22:2) While there is no way of knowing what our Lord wrote on the ground, the Law of Moses commanded the Jews to stone both the man and the woman caught in adultery. So where was the adulterous man?

If the woman was *"caught in adultery,"* the man would have been there as well. (John 8:3) It seems purposeful that the Pharisees dragged only her to Jesus. The Pharisees would have known the Law. They were attempting to set a trap for Jesus, and the Adulterous Woman was their pawn. (John 8:6)

Selectivity is often the case when it comes to accusations of guilt. In this case, the behavior of the Pharisees was not only malicious but also deceitful. Why was the man not present? Was the adulterer a Pharisee; was he one of them? The Bible was silent on the man's whereabouts and on who he was.

The Pharisees continued to interrogate Jesus, until finally He stood up and made a statement of His own, *"Let anyone of you who is without sin be the first to throw a stone at her."* (John 8:7) Jesus created a situation in which they were caught in a web of their own making and had to retreat. The guilt they wished upon Jesus (and the woman) now fell upon themselves as they withdrew from His presence. Jesus forgave the woman and warned her to sin no more. He also exposed the Pharisees' selective application of the Scripture, and ultimately, where they stood before God. The Adulterous Woman's story was one in which God's grace overcame guilt and the penalty for guilt through the direct intervention of Jesus.

The definition of guilt is: "The fact of having committed a specified or implied offense or crime."[29] Humiliation comes from the feeling of being exposed and having our faults put on display for all to see. The fear of punishment or rejection as a result of the exposure can be overwhelming.

In the early '70s, there was a Japanese movie called *Female Prisoner #701*. The synopsis details the life of a miserable woman who was tricked and abused terribly by the man she loved and later by multiple men. It is a story of revenge and heartbreak. This Japanese film also served as an inspiration for Quentin Tarantino's movie *Kill Bill*.

The following song plays in *Female Prisoner #701*, and so when writing this chapter, I looked up the English translation. The lyrics make me think of the situation in which the Adulterous Woman found herself:

> *You're beautiful, you're the flower, he praises you.*
> *But if you bloom, he will get you scattered.*
> *Stupid. So stupid.*
> *I go so stupid singin' my grudge blues.*

---

[29]https://www.lexico.com/en/definition/guilt

You can accept your pitiful fate.
But when you cry, he'll make you cry more.
Women, oh women,
It's women's tears that makes my grudge blues...

They say it's a dream,
Embers of one-sided attachment, laughing at you.
So you decide to wake up, but fear to be fully awake.
Women, oh women,
Women's soul beats on my grudge blues...

No flower would bloom on my dead body.
So I will live along hanging on my grudge.
Women, oh women,
My woman's life belongs to my grudge blues.[30]

There is a rawness in the lyrics as the singer laments over her situation. Like the Adulterous Woman, she has been "taken advantage of." Seemingly, a bitterness grew deep in her heart from the unfairness of her situation. The Adulterous Woman had been caught in a sinful relationship with a man who did not value truth over sin… and she was the only one accused.

While this woman's guilt came about in the form of physical adultery, spiritual adultery - the act of being unfaithful to God - is even more devastating. There are many places in the Bible where we see how God is affected when His people abandon Him.

---

[30] Urami Bushi by Meiko Kaji

Christ and the Adulteress
Rodolfo Bernadelli (1884)

Perhaps there is no better parallel to describe how God feels about spiritual adultery than the story of Hosea and Gomer:

> *When the Lord first spoke to Israel through Hosea, He said to Hosea, "Go and get married; your wife will be unfaithful, and your children will be just like her. In the same way my people have left me and become unfaithful."* (Hosea 1:2 GNT)

By having Hosea marry Gomer, God taught Israel to understand the emotional trauma that He goes through when His people leave Him - committing spiritual adultery. He so earnestly desires a relationship with us that He makes

Himself entirely vulnerable to us. It is those we love deeply that hurt us the most because we have given them our hearts.

What makes God different is not the pain that He feels at being betrayed but His reaction to it. God is full of mercy and compassion. Even in the face of guilt, He can still forgive completely.

As a "guilty soul," when things happen that place me in a negative "spotlight," it is easy for me to feel the need to defend myself. In these times, Jesus' example should be our standard. When I have fallen short and feel like I am "in a fishbowl," I remember that I must entrust myself to God and be more humble like the Adulterous Woman. God took care of her, and He will always take care of you and me.

Let us digress for a moment: Do you remember our definition for guilt? Guilt is "the fact of having committed a specified or implied offense or crime." Particularly important to note: Guilt may or may not be accompanied by "guilty feelings." So, there are hard-hearted people who are guilty of committing horrific sins but they "feel no guilty feelings." Conversely, one can have unnecessary guilty feelings that linger from the past, yet God has already forgiven the guilt because of confession and repentance. (That is me!)

Truthfully, guilty feelings have a vital place in our lives. It should be a "light on the dashboard" that tells us our conscience is in distress. The healthy and godly purpose of guilty feelings is to urge us to confess and repent. This is when the "light on the dashboard" should shut off.

In the same way, anger, like guilty feelings, has a role. It is a light on the dashboard that tells us when others have sinned against us. It allows us to talk to those who hurt us in a respectful manner and resolve things. Sadly, when others do not want to repent, our anger can grow and become a problem. Anger tells us when someone else is in sin, and guilty feelings tell us when we are in sin. Both are useful but can become a problem if we cannot handle them spiritually. It is so important that we resolve our feelings of guilt and anger wholly and quickly.

When we fall short, we should be open with God in prayer and with sisters that we trust, then sincerely repent. *"The Lord is not slow to fulfill His promise as some count slowness, but is patient toward you, not wishing that any should perish, but that all should reach repentance."* (2 Peter 3:9 ESV) We must believe that when we repent, our sins are *"blotted out."* (Acts 3:19) That is why the Bible says, *"Because of the Lord's great love we are not consumed, for His compassions never fail. They are new every morning; great is your faithfulness."* (Lamentations 3:22-23)

Part of the solution to overcoming the Paper Tiger of Guilty Feelings is ownership. *"Whoever conceals his transgressions will not prosper, but he who confesses and forsakes them will obtain mercy."* (Proverbs 28:13 ESV) It takes nobility to take ownership. *"Why do you look at the speck of sawdust in your brother's eye and pay no attention to the plank in your own eye?"* (Matthew 7:3-5) What part of the situation can you own? Focus on that, and then help others.

We must believe that God can change anyone… including ourselves. Anyone can overcome their past if they go to God desiring such. Not only does God allow this, He expects this. *"Do not be conformed to this world, but be transformed by the renewal of your mind, that by testing you may discern what is the will of God, what is good and acceptable and perfect."* (Romans 12:2 ESV) God wants us to take ownership and be transformed and renewed. What an important part of dealing with guilt and the ensuing guilty feelings in a spiritual way. God wants us to change *"…that times of refreshing may come from the presence of the Lord."* (Acts 3:20)

On the other hand, Satan loves to cause us to feel unworthy and ashamed. *"For the accuser of our brothers and sisters, who accuses them before our God day and night, has been hurled down."* (Revelations 12:10) Like the Pharisees, Satan's words can echo in our minds over and over again, making us feel guilty unnecessarily. In reality, when we listen to Satan's lies, half-truths, and "old truths," we become Satan's hostages. Thankfully, Jesus remains unfazed. The price that justice demanded was already fulfilled by Christ almost 2,000 years ago.

The Adulterous Woman had likely been ensnared in sin for some time. However, her breaking point finally came when she was caught and dragged before Jesus. Imagine that moment and how she must have felt. The moment of guilt and even shame and humiliation can be a crossroads. It is a moment to turn to God and experience incredible change. We should not fear these moments, we should be ready to embrace them.

When the Adulterous Woman was finally alone with Jesus, she realized that her life has been spared. Jesus says, *"Then neither do I condemn you... go now and leave your life of sin."* (John 8:11) She was given another chance. Her near stoning was the Adulterous Woman's moment to have a "hard reset" of her life and live for God. Guilty feelings provide us the same opportunity as the Adulterous Woman to come "face to face" with Jesus and to receive the same forgiveness and the same chance to change.

When we fear shame and guilt, we are hard to disciple. This hurts our relationship with other women and our husbands. Often this leads to a "victim mentality." A victim mentality is often coupled with blame-shifting back on the person who is trying to help us. As women, we must have godly expectations to be discipled and want to learn and grow. When we rid ourselves of guilty feelings, we can decide to be coached - even when it is challenging or difficult to hear the truth.

It is not enough to understand forgiveness. We must decide to leave our life of sin.

> *For the grace of God has appeared that offers salvation to all people. It teaches us to say "No" to ungodliness and worldly passions, and to live self-controlled, upright and godly lives in this present age, while we wait for the blessed hope - the appearing of the glory of our great God and Savior, Jesus Christ, who gave Himself for us to redeem us from all wickedness and to purify for Himself a people*

> *that are His very own, eager to do what is good.*

(Titus 2:11-14)

It does us no good to fixate on the shortcomings of others; rather, we must have a spirit of mercy and truth, just like Jesus who is *"full of grace and truth."* (John 1:14) We must love people more than the relationship if we are going to successfully disciple them to maturity. As Paul shared, *"Him we proclaim, warning everyone and teaching everyone with all wisdom, that we may present everyone mature in Christ. For this I toil, struggling with all His energy that He powerfully works within me."* (Colossians 1:28-29 ESV)

In other words, we have the authority to help others to overcome. With Jesus, we all receive a second chance to turn our guilt into salvation. Discipling has not only saved my soul on repeated occasions, but my marriage as well. I am so thankful to those who gently *"spoke the truth in love"* to me when I was guilty of sin. (Ephesians 4:15) Praise God with repentance - every time - I left my life of sin.

Practically speaking, overcoming the Paper Tiger of Guilty Feelings is about not allowing ourselves to be crushed and condemned by the truth about our sins and shortcomings. Instead, we must allow the truth to change us to be more like Christ. As women, when we cannot receive correction without immediately bursting into tears, this indicates a profound pride. This worldly sorrow makes it impossible for those around us to disciple and correct us. (2 Corinthians 7:10)

Only by removing the focus from ourselves and setting our gaze on Jesus can we benefit fully from discipling. By allowing ourselves to be washed through the word, we can be presented to Christ *"without stain or wrinkle or any other blemish, but holy and blameless."* (Ephesians 5:27) We must remember that our conscience's pricking is meant to spur us, not tear us down.

This has been a challenging principle for me to learn. In the past, I fell into a form of false humility upon being discipled. Tears would flood my eyes at the smallest correction. I would "accept" discipling but would then be sullen. I was full of self-pity instead of being inspired to do better. I was not *"strong in the grace."* (2 Timothy 2:1) This lack of humility and the acceptance of grace came down to a lack of spiritual maturity. How we respond to discipling indicates our maturity level and does determine to what extent God can work through us. Do not let "discipling" give you a perpetual guilty feeling... simply repent!

To share openly, in writing this book, I received constructive criticism (discipling). My ensuing guilty feelings paralyzed me from writing for a long while. I felt defeated and not good enough. Then I saw that the discipling was out of love to help me to excel. So, I repented of holding on to my guilty feelings and started to write again. Now I really appreciate Kip, because he was just trying to make me the best writer that I could be!

As Christians, guilty feelings are redeeming, as they can be the catalyst of the great gift of a second chance! They offer us the beginning of the path to be better and to do better. Through repenting of our guilt and not holding on to our guilty feelings, God multiplies our talents and allows us to mature in Christ.

The Paper Tiger of Guilty Feelings is defeated by seeing guilt and guilty feelings for what they are. Guilt can only be erased by responding to the blood of Jesus. Guilty feelings are the thunderous orchestra of the angels conducted by the Holy Spirit asking us to search our heart regarding our guilt, while urging us to change. However, a guilty feeling must be a temporary guest, that once it has fulfilled its purpose, should be invited to leave. Do not be afraid of this guest, do not hate it, or shun it. Your guilt and your guilty feelings are not who you are… You are a daughter and princess of the Creator of the Universe.

"Sometimes it takes a heartbreak to shake us awake and help us see we are worth so much more than we are settling for."

Mandy Hale

Paper Tiger Seven
Naomi's Bitterness

Naomi and her Daughters
George Dawe (1804)

In the days when the Judges ruled, there was a famine in the land. So a man from Bethlehem in Judah, together with his wife and two sons, went to live for a while in the country of Moab. The man's name was Elimelek, his wife's name was Naomi, and the names of his two sons

> were Mahlon and Kilion. They were Ephrathites from Bethlehem, Judah. And they went to Moab and lived there.
>
> Now Elimelek, Naomi's husband, died, and she was left with her two sons. They married Moabite women, one named Orpah and the other Ruth. After they had lived there about ten years, both Mahlon and Kilion also died, and Naomi was left without her two sons and her husband. (Ruth 1:1-5)

During the time of the Judges, Naomi and her husband, a dignitary from Bethlehem called Elimelech, fled from Judea on account of the famine in the land. They took their two young sons with them and set out to find a better situation in which to live. After settling in Moab for a while, Naomi was then faced with one of a wife's greatest fears; her husband Elimelech died. However, her sons married - Kilion to Orpah and Mahlon to Ruth.

Some Jewish scholars believe that the silence in the Bible about Elimelech and his two sons indicates disfavor. In the *Ruth Rabbah* - an exegetical homiletic interpretation of the *Book of Ruth* - Elimelech is described as a man fleeing Canaan. He did not flee because he would be in danger of suffering due to the famine, but because he did not want to be approached and called upon to help assuage the suffering of his fellow man.[31]

---

[31] https://en.wikipedia.org/wiki/Ruth_(biblical_figure)

Whatever the reason, gone was Naomi's partner in life, her husband, who provided for her. Her only solace should have become her sons, their wives and children - who would eventually come from these unions. For women in Biblical times, having sons would have meant being blessed and that the family name would continue. At the very least, Naomi could look forward to safety and security in the houses of her sons and precious grandchildren to bring her joy in the later years of her life.

Then a second horrific tragedy occurs: Both of Naomi's sons seemingly die at about the same time. Naomi was left without anyone to carry on the family name. During these days, for a woman to lose both her husband and her sons would have been interpreted as a curse, and that God was unhappy with her.

Without men to provide for her, a widow would be left exposed to the brutality of the world. As she was an older woman, her choices would have been narrowed down even further. She may eventually have been reduced to being a beggar. An equally terrible fate might have been expected for her daughters-in-law if they had stayed with her. Naomi, desperate to provide a practical solution, urged her daughters-in-law to return to their families. In her mind, Naomi felt there was a better chance for marriage for the daughters-in-laws with their families.

For Naomi, this was a time of intense heartache. Orpah refuses at first to return to her family, but she eventually obeyed her mother-in-law and left. Ruth, however, remained steadfast in her resolve.

> "Look," said Naomi, "your sister-in-law is going back to her people and her gods. Go back with her."
>
> But Ruth replied, "Don't urge me to leave you or to turn back from you. Where you go I will go, and where you stay I will stay. Your people will be my people and your God my God. Where you die I will die, and there I will be buried. May the Lord deal with me, be it ever so severely, if even death separates you and me." When Naomi realized that Ruth was determined to go with her, she stopped urging her. (Ruth 1:15-18)

This is the only time in the entire book that we see Ruth disobey her mother-in-law. The Bible describes Ruth as being *"determined to go with her."* The definition of the word determined is, "having made a firm decision and being resolved not to change it." Ruth would not abandon her mother-in-law in her time of need.

Naomi and Ruth continued on their journey until they reached Bethlehem. Depending on the area of Moab in which they began to go to Bethlehem, they most likely would have traveled along the shores of the Dead Sea before entering the desert. This would have given Naomi time to think about her life and lament over her recent tragedies. During her time in Moab, Naomi was transformed by tragedy. It is no wonder that, upon her arrival in Bethlehem, she was virtually unrecognizable.

> *So the two women went on until they came to Bethlehem. When they arrived in Bethlehem, the whole town was stirred because of them, and the women exclaimed, "Can this be Naomi?"*
>
> *"Don't call me Naomi," she told them. "Call me Mara, because the Almighty has made my life very bitter. I went away full, but the Lord has brought me back empty. Why call me Naomi? The Lord has afflicted me; the Almighty has brought misfortune upon me."*
> (Ruth 1: 19-21)

Naomi's lament is heartbreaking. In Hebrew, Naomi means "pleasant, lovely and winsome" and the meaning of "Mara" is "bitter." When Naomi left Bethlehem, she had everything she desired and needed, and now, after suffering intense hardships, she returned, in her mind, *"empty."* For Naomi, God had stripped her of everything. God, however, does His best work when situations are at their worst.

Often, we read this passage of Scripture and make a generalized assumption that Naomi was in sin. She was bitter, which we typically interpret as a bad thing. While bitterness is classically considered bad, the meaning in the context of the Scripture may surprise you. An online article on the topic has this to say about the Biblical meaning of bitterness:

> The Scriptural meaning of the word *"bitterness" (MARA in Hebrew)* is different than the Western definition. In the Western

mindset, bitterness is a negative emotion or attitude in response to some perceived unfairness resulting in deep cynicism and pessimism.

However, the true Biblical meaning is that *"bitterness"* is literally the opposite of *"sweetness."* And this *"bitterness"* can be both tangible and poetic. It refers to an unbearable pain or difficult situation caused by a third party from which there appears to be no escape.[32]

This helps shed light on Naomi's words: She is undergoing unbearable pain and anguish. To lose husband, children and one daughter-in-law is more than most women can emotionally bear. Being a godly woman, Naomi believed God to be sovereign and so knew that God had allowed these events to transpire. She cannot escape her situation and must therefore endure it.

In our Western mindset, this is an exceedingly difficult concept with which to wrestle. When we feel bitterness, we can grapple with feelings of guilt, as though we should not feel this way. Therefore in an attempt to "repent," we fail to deal with our emotions in the right way and we do not heal.

We miss out on the spiritual lessons that can be gleaned from difficult situations. Biblically, bitterness is not always sin, just as anger is not always sin. For example in Ephesians 4:26, the Bible teaches, ***"In your anger do not sin."*** What

---

[32]https://messianic-revolution.com/e17-1-the-modern-western-definition-of-bitterness-is-different-than-the-biblical-meaning/

we choose to do with bitterness is what matters. Bitter moments are a spiritual "fork in the road." We can choose to either focus on our bitter situation and then become sinfully bitter... or we can rely on God to become a better Christian. (Hebrews 12:7-15)

Consider the following Scriptures on bitterness:

"In her deep anguish Hannah prayed to the Lord, weeping bitterly." (1 Samuel 1:10) Hannah's bitter weeping moved God to grant her the desires of her heart and give her a son. Hannah's bitterness drew her to God, and God to her. *"The Lord is close to the brokenhearted and saves those who are crushed in spirit."* (Psalm 34:18)

When God saw the bitter affliction of His people, He sent Moses. The people were not in sin because they suffered bitterly. This signaled to God that they were ready for a deliverer, Moses.

> *The Lord said, "I have indeed seen the misery of my people in Egypt. I have heard them crying out because of their slave drivers, and I am concerned about their suffering. So I have come down to rescue them from the hand of the Egyptians...*
>
> *So now, go. I am sending you [Moses] to Pharaoh to bring my people the Israelites out of Egypt."* (Exodus 3:7-10)

King David wrote about the bitterness in his life. He said, *"Though you have made me see troubles, many and bitter, you will restore my life again; from the depths of the Earth you will again bring me up."* (Psalm 71:20) God is "beckoned" by our righteous response to "bitter events." David's bitter trials made him stronger, more righteous, and more connected to God.

"Then Peter remembered the word Jesus had spoken: 'Before the rooster crows, you will disown me three times.' And he went outside and wept bitterly." (Matthew 26:75) The bitter tears of Peter were "good" as they signaled brokenness. He cried bitter tears because of the gravity of his sin.

Conversely, unhealed bitterness that is not taken to God can be extremely dangerous. *"Get rid of all bitterness, rage and anger, brawling and slander, along with every form of malice."* (Ephesians 4:31) Notice the pairings in this Scripture. Bitterness, when paired with rage, anger, fighting, slander and malice, becomes a deadly poison.

We must be honest with God and with other disciples about the hurt that comes into our life. The Bible teaches, *"Each heart knows its own bitterness, and no one else can share its joy."* (Proverbs 14:10) No one goes very long in this sinful world without bitter experiences. Biblically, bitterness can be fuel. On the one hand, it can power our prayer life and signal God a need for help or a need for deep repentance. It also allows others to support and help us, strengthening our relationships.

Similarly, unhealed bitterness can begin to take root if left in the heart for too long. Once bitterness attaches itself to our heart, it can then make us and those around us spiritually sick. *"See to it that no one falls short of the grace of God and that no bitter root grows up to cause trouble and defile many."* (Hebrews 12:15) Bitterness can fuel your spiritual life, or it can be mixed with resentment and self-pity to cause devastating damage.

One of the worst things we can do with bitterness is to try to sedate it or *"...boast about it or deny the truth."* (James 3:14) Regardless of what we try to medicate to cover the pain of bitterness - impurity, food, drunkenness or even prescribed medicine - deep-rooted bitterness will eventually come back up to the surface. This is not to say that disciples should not use prescribed medication properly; however, spiritual problems cannot be solved medically. The best solution to eliminate bitterness is to draw closer to God. When we acknowledge our "hurts" and cry out to Him, He will heal our hearts.

> *Listen to my words, Lord, consider my lament. Hear my cry for help, my King and my God, for to you I pray.*
>
> *In the morning, Lord, you hear my voice; in the morning I lay my requests before you and wait expectantly.* (Psalm 5:1-3)

Another important lesson in overcoming the Paper Tiger of Bitterness, we should learn from Naomi. When we are "hit" by a bitter experience, we can all use a "Ruth" in our life. We need someone determined to stay by our side, for *"a *friend loves at all times, and a [sister] is born for adversity."* (Proverbs 17:17 ESV) Naomi did not realize this as she had urged Ruth to leave her, but God would not allow her to be isolated and all alone in her suffering.

Naomi's partnership with Ruth was an integral part of God's plan. In having to care and be concerned for Ruth, it provides meaning and a future for Naomi. Alone, the bitterness Naomi experienced would have taken root, and her story would have ended. Instead, because Ruth refused to leave her, Naomi's growing love for Ruth kept her going. After returning to Bethlehem, Naomi slowly overcame her bitterness. She began to turn her attention to the situation at hand and even gets proactive to find a special someone for Ruth. She comes up with a plan:

> *One day Ruth's mother-in-law Naomi said to her, "My daughter, I must find a home for you, where you will be well provided for. Now Boaz, with whose women you have worked, is a relative of ours. Tonight he will be winnowing barley on the threshing floor.* (Ruth 3:1-2)

Naomi had a debt of gratitude toward Ruth for not leaving her, and in turn, Ruth had a debt of gratitude toward Naomi for sustaining her. (Ruth 2:1-19) Since a mutual trust developed, Ruth agreed to do whatever Naomi said:

> *Wash, put on perfume, and get dressed in your best clothes. Then go down to the threshing floor, but don't let him know you are there until he has finished eating and drinking. When he lies down, note the place where he is lying.*

> *Then go and uncover his feet and lie down. He will tell you what to do."*
>
> *"I will do whatever you say," Ruth answered. So she went down to the threshing floor and did everything her mother-in-law told her to do.* (Ruth 3:3-6)

For Naomi, there was no time for half measures; the plan must be bold if it was going to work. The plan - which bordered on outright seduction - had Ruth wash, put on perfume, be dressed in her best clothes, and go to the threshing floor to take note of where Boaz would fall asleep. Then Ruth was to rush over as quietly as possible, uncover his feet, and lie down. The next morning, Ruth returned to Naomi and told her what happened:

> *When Ruth came to her mother-in-law, Naomi asked, "How did it go, my daughter?"*
>
> *Then she told her everything Boaz had done for her and added, "He gave me these six measures of barley, saying, 'Don't go back to your mother-in-law empty-handed.'"*
>
> *Then Naomi said, "Wait, my daughter, until you find out what happens. For the man will not rest until the matter is settled today."* (Ruth 3: 16-18)

Naomi was a strategist. Her plan worked so well that Boaz was utterly smitten. He sent a generous gift back to Naomi out of respect and care. Though the Scriptures do not reveal all of Boaz's thoughts, perhaps Boaz was intrigued by this Moabite widow because his mother was none-other-than Rahab, the former prostitute. Interestingly, Rahab was a Canaanite who married the Jewish hero Salmon. Tradition holds that he was one of the two spies that Rahab saved. Indeed, Naomi's masterful advice and direction was about to change Boaz's and Ruth's lives forever.

In Eastern cultures, it was permitted for the servant to lay crosswise at the feet of their master. Also, customary was the availing by the servant of the coverings at the feet of their master. It was a way of signaling loyalty and submission.[33] This humble action - paired with the fact that Ruth smelled good and looked beautiful - communicated to Boaz the pure and godly desires of Ruth's heart.

This is powerful. Naomi and Ruth worked together to win the heart of Boaz. Naomi provided the plan, direction and the negotiations, and Ruth provided the transparency, obedience and action. There was no competition and no resentment. Both women knew their survival was at stake.

How does this apply to us? Every disciple will go through difficult times spiritually that are not "sweet," and therefore bitter. We can think that because we are going through pain, God has abandoned us. Thank God for Ruth, a young woman who refused to be "sent away," but instead loved Naomi enough to restore her faith in God that she could be used once more.

---

[33]https://www.biblestudytools.com/commentaries/jamieson-fausset-brown/ruth/ruth-3.html

Trusting God and making a decision to give our hearts after heartache is difficult, but like Jesus, we are called to take on *"the very nature of a servant"* and lay down our lives for one another. (Philippians 2:7) God is faithful. As He did for Naomi, He will renew our faith and hope once more.

Naomi did not call Ruth her daughter-in-law after Ruth's husband Mahlon had died, but *"daughter."* (Ruth 1:11) A child does not have to be biologically yours for you to love them as your own. Ruth became Naomi's daughter, not by birth but by decision. In turn, Ruth bound herself to Naomi in an unconditional way. Her loyalty transended Naomi's state of bitterness.

Ruth in Boaz's Field
Julius Schnorr von Carolsfeld (1828)

Their "teamwork" resulted in both Naomi and Ruth gaining more than they could have ever imagined. All of this was possible because Ruth made herself an "apprentice" to Naomi, and Naomi put all of her teachings into Ruth.

This is an important conviction for young women seeking discipling from older women: Our loyalty should not be conditional. After all, as you grow closer to a person, you see them during their "lows" as well as their "highs." It is a temptation of the Devil to become critical when we see our discipler in one of their lesser moments. As Christians, we are loyal to God and we trust that He will always work *"for the good of those who love Him."* (Romans 8:28) As a result, we entrust ourselves to flawed and imperfect people.

Ruth knew who Naomi really was. Naomi was not her bitter circumstances. Ruth believed in Naomi and what she had to offer, and so was able to weather the storms of Naomi's healing. Naomi's advice set forth a series of events that led to Ruth marrying Boaz.

> *So Boaz took Ruth and she became his wife. When he made love to her, the Lord enabled her to conceive, and she gave birth to a son. The women said to Naomi: "Praise be to the Lord, who this day has not left you without a guardian-redeemer. May he become famous throughout Israel! He will renew your life and sustain you in your old age. For your daughter-in-law, who loves you and who is better to you than seven sons, has given him birth."*
>
> *Then Naomi took the child in her arms and cared for him. The women living there said, "Naomi has a son!" And they named him Obed. He was the father of Jesse, the father of David.* (Ruth 4:13-17)

In our discipling relationships, we have to ask ourselves, are we like Orpah or Ruth? For Orpah, she looked after her own wellbeing. Ruth understood that she could be a great help to Naomi, and in time, Naomi proved an even greater blessing for Ruth... a protective husband and a beautiful baby named Obed.

As Naomi held Ruth's newborn baby, her heart must have been so full. Not long before, Naomi had been husbandless and childless, but now she had gained a son in Boaz, a daughter in Ruth, and grandson in Obed. Interestingly the Bible says that Obed was like a son to Naomi! Together, Naomi and Ruth had been able to find a situation that restored their joy and their place in society.

The Scriptures make mention of Obed for a significant reason: He was King David's grandfather. Even more amazing is that Jesus, the Son of God, was a direct descendant of David. In fact, most scholars believe that the *Book of Ruth* was written to show that God in His sovereignty "looked past" David's Moabite ancestry. (Deuteronomy 23:3)

What can the partnership of two women devoted to one another accomplish? That partnership can result in being used by God to bring about the salvation of multitudes. Together they change the world. That is the power of overcoming the Paper Tiger of Bitterness.

I am so grateful for the "Ruths" that are in my life today. One very special Ruth is Sarah Dimitry. Sarah is a woman that I admire for her boldness in preaching the gospel, her transparency in confessing her sin, and her love for the Kingdom. Sarah and I have been partners in the gospel for over a decade. I have had the honor of seeing her become a wife, a first-time mother, a Women's Ministry Leader and a Geographic Sector Leader. I recently witnessed her walk across the stage to become one of the first women to receive the prestigious International College of Christian Ministries Master's Degree.

The Author is so grateful for her dear friend Sarah!

As Jason and Sarah are close friends to Tim and me, so encouraging is that our children are great friends too. I am grateful for her leadership in the DREAM Geographic Sector as she leads the women in their walk with God.

In Los Angeles, it is such a joy to see Karen Gregory grow to become such an outstanding Women's Ministry Leader overseeing the CORE Super Region and the IGNITE Teen Corps. Her hard work ethic and servant's heart are such an encouragement to so many. Karen is true family. I cannot imagine life in Los Angeles without her.

Similar words can be said for Elizabeth McDonnell. Elizabeth has done so much for God as a missionary in the Philippines, and as a church leader in the United States. As a mother of four, I have the utmost respect for her as she is one of the most spiritually disciplined women I have had the pleasure of knowing. She powerfully leads the Alpha and Omega Super Region in Los Angeles alongside her incredible husband, Richie.

Joey and Karen Gregory celebrate after being pronounced "husband and wife!"

Elizabeth and the Author in Manila at the Pacific Rim Missions Conference in 2018.

April Baker is a "Ruth" that came into my life fairly recently. I appreciate her heroic leadership while enduring a severe condition associated with her physical heart. April leads the All 4 One Super Region alongside RD, her awesome husband. April's and my strengths and weaknesses complement each other. It has been such a joy to work together on the 2021 Women's Day.

RD and April Baker planted the Dubai International Christian Church in 2016.

Joaly Carr is another incredible "Ruth" in my life. I have so many fond memories working side by side with Joaly to usher women into the waters of baptism. She is truly a joy, and I am so grateful for her leadership in the Revolution Super Region. Of note, Joaly has trained and appointed so many other Women's Ministry Leaders.

Joaly is an incredible wife, mother and Women's Ministry Leader!

Another delightful and impressive Ruth is Coleen Challinor. I am so proud of Coleen's maturity in Christ at such a young age. This translates directly into her dynamic leadership of the Southeast Asia Geographic Sector.

The Author and her dear "International Ruth" of Manila, Coleen!

Naomi's and Ruth's relationship has become a model to me as a "Naomi" and as a "Ruth." Today, the Region Leaders, Sector Leaders and Shepherdesses of the City of Angels Church have formed a powerful female leadership team. We are learning what it means to have the roles of "Naomi" and "Ruth."

> *Older women likewise are to be reverent in behavior, not slanderers or slaves to much wine. They are to teach what is good, and so train the young women to love their husbands and children, to be self-controlled, pure, working at home, kind, and submissive to their own husbands, that the word of God may not be reviled.* (Titus 2:3-5 ESV)

This dynamic between Naomi and Ruth, the older woman training the younger, is what we would today refer to as female discipleship. I found a fascinating article on female mentorship:

> A 2017 study found that 54% of women have access to senior female mentors throughout their career. The majority of older potential mentors, very few had ever been approached. In addition to this, 1 in 5 admitted to never having ever been approached.
>
> Interestingly, those numbers are not driven by a lack of older more mature women who desire to mentor, in fact the survey revealed that 71% of women would always accept the opportunity to mentor. There is a myth that executive females do not have time to mentor anyone, only 1 in 10 women decline the opportunity to mentor someone. Another myth is that men reap more benefits from mentorship interactions.

Lastly the myth that is easier to access a male mentor over a female is not entirely inaccurate. 67% of women rate mentorship as highly important.[34]

The role of Naomi, or female mentor in someone's life, is a vulnerable position. Being Naomi carries with it great risk, which is why true and long term female mentorship is hard to come by. An indicator may be found in Orpah's response to Naomi. When Naomi tells her to go home, she does. She does not fight it. Simultaneously, the Bible does record her crying, indicating there was a closeness in their relationship. Conversely, Ruth was bold enough to insist that Naomi accept her.

The first "Naomi" that I ever had was my incredible mother. As a child, I was brought up between two cultures: Canadian and Trinidadian. Being able to benefit from two amazing cultures was a blessing. Having the privilege of growing up in Canada is something I appreciate more and more as I have had the opportunity to travel the world for the gospel.

My mother left Trinidad as a young woman to be a modern dancer in Canada. I remember watching her dance in productions and being overwhelmed with pride. My mother

---

[34]https://www.forbes.com/sites/falonfatemi/2018/05/15/four-myths-that-perpetuate-the-scarcity-of-female-mentor-mentee-relationships/

was beautiful, elegant and graceful as she danced. In my eyes, there was nothing that she could not do.

The Author and her beloved mother and loving stepfather!

Born and raised in Canada - supported by a loving single mom alongside an incredibly hardworking stepfather - my life was very comfortable. We were not rich by any means, but we had everything we needed, and most of the time, everything we wanted!

My mother was a "Proverbs 31 Woman" when it came to her creativity. She made and designed clothes, as well as cooking and catering scrumptious Trinidadian food. Whatever she saw, she could replicate. I am convinced that I get my artistic gifts from her, along with my love for all things DIY (Do It Yourself). I would not be the woman I am today if it were not for my mother and stepfather's impact in my life. I will always remember my mother's laughter and her love and affection for me.

For me, very sadly, on December 14, 2020, my dear mother passed away. In the days leading up to my mother's death, I began writing letters. I know she would never be able to read them but expressing the emotions that I was going through helped me cope with the reality that I would lose this woman who had been such an important person in my life.

After getting off of the phone with the doctor and hearing that my mother now had six hours to live, I wrote the following:

Mom,

I am preparing myself now. Brian is going to call and then I will see you for the last time. I am nervous. My stomach is in knots. I am trying to keep calm.

I love you.

If I don't get out the words right, then at least I want to say them to you here. I love you, Mom.

Thank you for being my mom. Thank you for carrying me, loving me, and taking care of me. Thank you for teaching me to love God. Thank you for bringing Fabian as well as Brian into our lives.

Thank you for everything that you have done for me. I am grateful. I was blessed to have you as a mother.

I will miss you.

Thank you, thank you, thank you, Mom.

I love you.

Another "Naomi" was my dear stepmother, Brigitte. Brigitte passed on to my sisters and me all of the lessons that she had learned from her mother, one of the most elegant French women I have had the pleasure of meeting. Brigitte taught me how to knit, how to make French vinaigrette (something my own children benefit from to this day), and many other aspects of being a "joyful homemaker." Through her example, I strove to imitate the effortless elegance for which French women are known.

Another Naomi in my life is my mother-in-law, Eleanor. Eleanor has been an incredible grandmother to my boys, and I am forever grateful for her presence in their lives. Her care and generosity have given my sons - more often than not - the "desires of their hearts." Thank you, Eleanor, for being such a generous and constant presence in our lives!

The Author and her family so adore "Gwamma" Eleanor!

Other "Naomis" that I had early on in my spiritual life are Anne Demougin, Helen Luzine and Gillianne Brisebois. God used these Women's Ministry Leaders to shape me and build in me a solid spiritual foundation. Anne studied the Bible with me. I would not be here today if it were not for those times of Bible study. God used her to bring me out of the darkness and into the light.

Helen taught me to ask lots of questions. The more questions that you ask when you are ministering to a person, the more accurate your use of the Scriptures in their life will be. She taught me the importance of listening. The first person I had the honor of discipling - as a six-month-old disciple - was because Helen empowered me, even though I was an immature Christian.

Gillianne taught me that a Women's Ministry Leader could be spiritual... and funny. Gillianne taught me how to be comfortable in my own skin and down to Earth. As a young disciple, I looked up to her so much and wanted to be just like her. Gillianne's lighthearted and cheerful example is now the spirit of what I strive to bring to my ministry.

Continuing on, other important "Naomi's" in my life are Therese Untalan, Denise Bordieri and Sharon Kirchner. Therese is someone that I can say anything to and with whom I feel completely safe. She knows the worst about me and yet has taught me the importance of having a pure heart. Therese has been there during some of my darkest moments, and she always thinks of plans that will help keep me close to God.

Coleen, Therese and the Author at the
ICCM Gala in Los Angeles in 2019.

Denise - a cancer survivor - taught me to persevere even when times were difficult. She is an honest and trustworthy relationship in my life. Denise is a woman with whom I can share vulnerably, someone who will validate what I am feeling and yet not allow bitterness to take root in my heart.

Denise and the Author at the MERCY Orphanage
in Phnom Penh, Cambodia.

Sharon - another awesome Naomi that God brought into my life - has taught me the importance of prayer and to lean on God. Sharon will call and pray with me, ask me how I am doing, and urge me to turn to God in everything. She is an extraordinary example of compassion and love.

The Kernans celebrated Sharon's birthday alongside Sharon's husband, Michael.

Another pivotal Naomi that came into my life in 2017 was Emma Causey. The first time we met was in the City of Angels Church West Region Women's Day. As Elena's guest, she had worked as a Women's Ministry Leader and partner in the gospel for many years with the McKeans alongside her awesome husband, John. Emma and I became instant friends.

Over the past three years, I have had the pleasure of knowing Emma, and she has changed my life in so many ways. Her partnership in the gospel has met a need in me that I did not think I had. I have learned so much from both John and Emma as they valiantly helped Tim and me lead the mighty City of Angels Church.

Of all of the women who have passed through LA that I have had the pleasure of working with side by side, I cried the most over Emma's departure. Her experience in the ministry for so many years along with her example of love and respect for Elena remain an upward call.

On John's and Emma's last day as members of the LA Staff, I had this to share about Emma:

> Judges 4:4-9 DEV (Disciple Encouragement Version. Disclaimer: Not to be mistaken with the Word of God of course, but encouraging in its own way.)
>
> At that time, Emma the prophetess, wife of John, served as Women's Ministry Leader over the City of Angels Women's Ministry. She used to sit beside Lianne, situated in the front row at staff, between her husband John and Lianne, and the women would go up to her there to settle disputes and seek advice.
>
> She urgently sent for Lianne, the wife of Tim, out of Canada. Emma said, the Eternal God of Israel commands you: "Go and get into position. Take your LA Women's Staff with you and impact Los Angeles. I will help you and be a comfort to you as you grow into your role, and God will work powerfully." Lianne said to Emma, "I will do this if you will go with me."
>
> Emma said, "I will certainly go with you, but you should know from the beginning that this battle will not lead to anyone's personal glory. The Eternal has decreed that the victory will go to the unity and

partnership of the entire women's ministry, and consequently, the church." Then Emma got up and went to Chicago, after having accompanied Lianne for the past three years.

Thank you, Emma for your courage to persevere and to give your heart fully to me. As a woman who has sacrificed and fought many battles for God in the ministry, has raised incredible children, and who has been such an exemplary wife, I am forever grateful. I am deeply honored to be considered your sister in Christ, your friend and also one of your "Ruths." I want you to know that is how I see you.

Emma and the Author during the 2019 Women's Day in Los Angeles.

Last and certainly not least, a woman who has been the most like Naomi to me is Dr. Elena Garcia McKean. Elena is an incredibly faithful woman of God. Throughout her 44-year marriage with Kip, God has unfolded His incredible plan for her life. No one understands completely the struggles that I face in my leadership role quite like Elena.

As she wrote in her book, *Elevate - Jesus' Global Revolution For Women*, her life and ministry are not without the bitterness of soul that comes through difficulty and tragedy. Some situations have caused heaviness and emotional fatigue in her life. She had poured her life's blood into building the Kingdom of God in the '80s and '90s only to see Satan infiltrate and tear it to pieces from the inside.

Elena shared that she was tempted to feel abandoned as there were many "Orpahs" that turned back. As well, Elena could have felt like God's hand was against her, and the ministry was just simply "too much." Instead, she clung to her God and allowed new "Ruths" to cling to her and revive her faith.

I know that when God brought Elena and me together, it must have been a scary moment for her. How do any of us give our hearts and trust again after such pain? How do we invest in young women once more? How do we pour our heart and faith out once more, knowing full well that the women to whom we are giving could turn their back on us as well and abandon us?

For most, other than Elena, the cost of investing in others again was just too high. There was so much bitterness and disappointment in these battle-weary sisters, and consequently, they no longer had the heart for world evangelism. There can be a fear in our hearts when it comes to trusting again after bitter experiences… especially in ministry. Elena's singular faith, hope and love overcame the Paper Tiger of Bitterness.

Elena's book *Elevate* is a "must-read" for every disciple, both men and women!

There is a powerful song in the popular musical - *Les Miserables* - that perfectly illustrates this Naomi-like pain that comes from the tragic loss of relationships:

There's a grief that can't be spoken,
There's a pain goes on and on.
Empty chairs at empty tables,
Now my friends are dead and gone.

Here they talked of revolution,
Here it was they lit the flame,
Here they sang about tomorrow
And tomorrow never came.

From the table in the corner,
They could see a world reborn,
And they rose with voices ringing,
And I can hear them now
The very words that they have sung
Became their last communion
On this lonely barricade, at dawn.

Oh my friends, my friends forgive me
That I live and you are gone
There's a grief that can't be spoken,
And there's a pain goes on and on

Phantom faces at the window,
Phantom shadows on the floor,
Empty chairs at empty tables
Where my friends will meet no more.
Oh my friends, my friends don't ask me
What your sacrifice was for
Empty chairs at empty tables
Where my friends will sing no more.

The pain of seeing friends and family turn away from God leaves scars in a person's heart that are hard to explain. What's more, this emotional abandonment makes it more difficult for those innocent people who come along with a desire to become "Ruths" to these women.

Elena let me in. She had a plan for me. Her desire to make sure that I have a women's ministry to belong to where I can be emotionally and spiritually provided for has given me so much.

Elena surrounded by her "Ruths" - the World Sector Women's Ministry Leaders!

In the same way, I know that she needed me. "Through thick and thin," I have continued to cling to her because I want her to see God's love through my loyalty and respect.

As she has healed me in so many ways, I pray that I too have been able to help heal her old wounds.

A Naomi and a Ruth relationship is a spiritual partnership. Without a more mature woman like Elena discipling me, there are so many more mistakes that I would have made in leadership. I did not decide to become a "Ruth" to Elena because she is perfect. I was determined to be a "Ruth" to her because we are spiritual family and I feel called by God to do so. God always has a plan for all of us, even in our darkest moments. In light of my mother's recent passing, Elena has become my mother now more than ever because of the Holy Spirit burning inside of us.

The Author and her "Naomi," Elena!

I want her to know that as my teacher, her sacrifices, her heartbreak, her hard work and her perseverance have and continue to bear fruit in me. *"Nevertheless, the one who receives instruction in the word should share all good things with their instructor."* (Galatians 6:6) I want her to find joy when she sees the women raised up under my care and know that they would not be what they are today without her presence in my life. She is my "Naomi."

The splendor of the story of Naomi and Ruth is that Ruth refused to be turned away. And so it should be with our worldwide sisterhood. God used the bitterness of loss to give birth to this extraordinary partnership between mentor and apprentice. An impossible situation was turned around and brought about two lives of great fulfillment and eternal destiny. God wants to do the same with each of us.

One final encouragement: While Orpah turned back and was never heard from again, that does not need to be where the story ends for us. For those who have "turned back," God can provide a path to return once more to cling, not only to Him, but to other spiritual women.

Incredible spiritual parents to the Author and her husband Tim - Kip and Elena!

The Paper Tiger of Bitterness wants us to give in, but we must resist. As the saying goes, "It is always darkest before the dawn." We must have the patience and trust in God to await the blessings that come with the first rays of sunlight. And to God be all the glory!

Epilogue

She is clothed in strength and dignity;
She can laugh at the days to come.
She speaks with wisdom,
And faithful instruction is on their tongue.
She watches over the affairs of her household
And does not eat the bread of idleness.
Her children arise and call her blessed;
Her husband also, and he praises her:
"Many women do noble things,
But you surpass them all."
Charm is deceptive, and beauty is fleeting;
But a woman who fears the Lord is to be praised.
Honor her for all that her hands have done,
And let her works bring her praise at the city gate. (Proverbs 31:25-31)

Who is the woman that has overcome the seven Paper Tigers that we have discussed? She is the woman described in Proverbs 31. A woman who is *"clothed in strength and dignity."* She is a woman, a suitable helper made by God, who can smile and find joy and contentment because she fully trusts in her Lord.

She is wise and is thoroughly equipped for *"teaching, rebuking, correcting and training in righteousness."* (2 Timothy 3:16) She cares for her household and ensures they have all they need. She is a trustworthy companion and confidant to her husband, as well as a loving and dutiful mother. In a word, she is noble.

She loves God deeply and is honored for her work near and far. She is to be admired, imitated and respected. Not because it was easy, but because she earned it through prayer and persevering in *"trials of many kinds."* (James 1:2)

Paper Tigers are merely that - paper. They are very real, but they are only as dangerous as we let them be. Amelia Earhart wrote:

> The most difficult thing is the decision to act, the rest is merely tenacity. The fears are paper tigers. You can do anything you decide to do. You can act to change and control your life; and the procedure, the process is its own reward.

Satan wants us to be terrified. He wants to "back us into a corner." He sends and will continue to send many Paper Tigers our way to catch us off guard, and we must be ready to face each one courageously.

Doubt preyed upon Sarah, but was scared away by the faith of Abraham. Desire for Control crept up on Rebekah, but was driven off by surrender. Rivalry crouched at Rachel's doorway, and friendship shut the door. Longing for the World growled at Lot's wife, but could have been overcome by gratitude. Suffering circled the Bleeding Woman, but was healed by vulnerability. Guilty Feelings roared at the Adulterous Woman, but grace shut its jaws. Bitterness pounced upon Naomi, but love and loyalty carried the day.

Try as they might, the Paper Tigers in our lives should have no power. We have looked at each obstacle through the lens of God's Word and have seen them for what they are.

Please do not give them power in your life. I hope and pray that together we can overcome all of the Paper Tigers, as we continue to spread the Kingdom of God around the world in THIS generation! And may the Lord continue to bless us individually and as a united sisterhood!

Contact The Author

Please feel free to email me with comments about this book and how it impacted you. Thank you.

lianne@usd21.org

The Author

Made in the USA
Las Vegas, NV
06 September 2021